D0082936

Hitler and the Rise of the Nazi Party

SEMINAR STUDIES IN HISTORY

Hitler and the Rise of the Nazi Party

FRANK McDONOUGH

PEARSON
Longman

London • New York • Toronto • Sydney • Tokyo • Singapore
Hong Kong • Cape Town • Madrid • Paris • Amsterdam • Munich • Milan

PEARSON EDUCATION LIMITED

Head Office:
Edinburgh Gate
Harlow CM20 2JE
Tel: +44 (0)1279 623623
Fax: +44 (0)1279 431059

London Office:
128 Long Acre
London WC2E 9AN
Tel: +44 (0)20 7447 2000
Fax: +44 (0)20 7447 2170
Website: www.history-minds.com

First published in Great Britain in 2003

© Pearson Education Limited 2003

The right of Frank McDonough to be identified as Author
of this Work has been asserted by him in accordance
with the Copyright, Designs and Patents Act 1988.

ISBN 0 582 50606 9

British Library Cataloguing in Publication Data
A CIP catalogue record for this book can be obtained from the British Library

Library of Congress Cataloging in Publication Data
A CIP catalog record for this book can be obtained from the Library of Congress

10 9 8 7 6 5 4 3 2 1

Typeset by 7 in 10/12 Sabon Roman
Produced by Pearson Education Asia Pte Ltd.
Printed and bound in Malaysia, LSP

The Publishers' policy is to use paper manufactured from sustainable forests.

For my Dad – with love

CONTENTS

INTRODUCTION TO THE SERIES

Such is the pace of historical enquiry in the modern world that there is an ever-widening gap between the specialist article or monograph, incorporating the results of current research, and general surveys, which inevitably become out of date. *Seminar Studies in History* is designed to bridge this gap. The series was founded by Patrick Richardson in 1966 and his aim was to cover major themes in British, European and world history. Between 1980 and 1996 Roger Lockyer continued his work, before handing the editorship over to Clive Emsley and Gordon Martel. Clive Emsley is Professor of History at the Open University, while Gordon Martel is Professor of International History at the University of Northern British Columbia, Canada, and Senior Research Fellow at De Montfort University.

All the books are written by experts in their field who are not only familiar with the latest research but have often contributed to it. They are frequently revised, in order to take account of new information and interpretations. They provide a selection of documents to illustrate major themes and provoke discussion, and also a guide to further reading. The aim of *Seminar Studies in History* is to clarify complex issues without over-simplifying them, and to stimulate readers into deepening their knowledge and understanding of major themes and topics.

ACKNOWLEDGEMENTS

We are indebted to the University of California Press for the reproduction of material from *The Weimar Republic Sourcebook* eds A. Kaes, M. Jay and E. Dimedberg, published by University of California Press 1994; and University of Exeter Press for the reproduction of material from *Nazism 1919–1945*, Vol 1: The Rise to Power 1919–1934 by J. Noakes and G. Pridham, published by University of Exeter Press 1983.

Photographs in the plate section are reproduced courtesy of Popperfoto.

In some instances we have been unable to trace the owners of copyright material, and we would appreciate any information that would enable us to do so.

CHRONOLOGY

1918

11 November Germany signs armistice to end First World War

1919

7 April Bavarian Soviet republic proclaimed in Munich (later suppressed by right-wing forces)

28 June Treaty of Versailles signed

September Adolf Hitler joins the German Workers' Party

1920

24 February Hitler announces new 25-point programme of the National Socialist German Workers' Party (NSDAP)

1921

29 July Adolf Hitler becomes undisputed leader of the Nazi Party

1922

18 July 'Law to protect the Republic' passed by the Reichstag

1923

11 January French and Belgian troops occupy the Ruhr to enforce payment of reparations. German government offers a policy of 'passive resistance'

Summer The 'great inflation' grips Germany, resulting in a complete collapse of the German Mark

26 September Kahr declares state of emergency in Bavaria

27 September President Ebert declares state of emergency throughout Germany

8 November Munich Beer Hall Putsch

1924

1 April Hitler sentenced to five years' detention for 'high treason' (released in December 1924)

9 August Dawes Plan on reparations payments announced

1925

28 February	President Ebert dies
27 April	Paul von Hindenburg, military figure from First World War, is elected as President
5 October	Locarno treaty signed

1926

| 8 September | Germany joins the League of Nations |

1927

| 31 January | The Allied military control mission is withdrawn from Germany |

1928

| 20 May | In the Reichstag elections, the Nazis poll a mere 2.8 per cent of total votes cast |

1929

| 3 October | Gustav Stresemann dies |
| 29 October | Wall Street stock market crash |

1930

| 30 March | Brüning appointed Chancellor |
| 14 September | The Nazi Party makes a spectacular breakthrough in the Reichstag elections, polling 18 per cent of votes, and holding 107 seats in the new parliament |

1932

10 April	Hindenburg re-elected President in run-off election against Adolf Hitler who polls 13 million votes
13 April	Hitler's Stormtroopers (SA) banned
30 May	Brüning resigns as Chancellor and is replaced by Franz von Papen
17 June	Ban on the SA is lifted
31 July	In the Reichstag elections, the Nazi Party polls 37.3 per cent of the total votes, holds 230 seats in the new parliament and is now the most popular party in Germany
6 November	In the second Reichstag elections of the year, the Nazi vote falls by 2 million and their seats in parliament fall to 196
17 November	Papen resigns as Chancellor
2 December	General von Schleicher is appointed Chancellor

1933

| 30 January | Adolf Hitler is appointed German Chancellor |

PART ONE

BACKGROUND

CHAPTER ONE

INTRODUCTION: THE CHANGING DEBATE

On 30 January 1933, Adolf Hitler was appointed Chancellor of Germany. In a very short space of time, he transformed Germany into a powerful, brutal and militaristic dictatorship. In September 1939, Hitler's dynamic foreign policy led to the outbreak of the Second World War, which eventually resulted in over 45 million unnecessary deaths, and horrific acts of genocide unparalleled in the annals of recorded history. In the aftermath of 'Hitler's War', most people wanted to know why all these catastrophic events had occurred. Historians looked for answers in Germany, not only by investigating the Nazi period, but also by examining the years before Hitler came to power, when Germany was still a democratic country.

The rise to power of Adolf Hitler and the Nazi Party is one of the most important events in the history of the twentieth century. In the immediate aftermath of the Second World War, historians not only investigated the evil deeds of the Nazi regime, but asked how Adolf Hitler could ever have been given power in the first place, within the seemingly democratic structure of Weimar Germany. The most popular and widely accepted interpretation suggested that Hitler had been 'jobbed into office' by the old authoritarian right at precisely the moment when the fragile popularity of the Nazi Party had peaked in democratic elections. In the view of Alan Bullock, and other non-German historians such as Lewis Namier, Hugh Trevor-Roper, William Shirer and A. J. P. Taylor, the democratic structure of Weimar Germany was far too reliant for survival on the reactionary forces of the right who had little sympathy with democracy and used Hitler as their willing agent to destroy it. Alan Bullock, Hitler's most celebrated biographer, claimed the collapse of democracy in Germany was indeed engineered by the authoritarian right, who believed Hitler could be tamed once in power, and then used to serve their own authoritarian ends. Of course, Bullock, a truly brilliant historian, knew he was writing 'contemporary history' in a period when emotion and moral outrage penetrated every pore of the historical debate. Hitler was naturally depicted as an 'evil genius' at best and a 'monster' at worst in most of the contemporary histories of the Nazi era, which became popular in the 1950s and early 1960s. It also became commonplace in this era for Nazism to be viewed as a backward-looking, negative and vague ragbag ideology which lacked any intellectual weight. This very understandable desire to confine National Socialism to a hermetically sealed time capsule and to portray Hitler as some sort of historical accident caused by bungling anti-democrats was influenced by the close proximity of the historians to the recent events of the Third Reich. Even though a historian should not be a 'hanging judge' when examining the past, it was, in fact, a rare occurrence in most of the early studies of Hitler and Nazism to find any historian willing to examine the rise and fall of the Third Reich with what could be termed 'objectivity'. The winners of the conflict were to write the historical verdict on Hitler and the Nazis and, as such, it was certain the losers would come off badly in the interpretations that were produced.

Another major problem with the historical debate on the Nazi period has been the extent to which it has been constrained by the prevailing political and international climate. In 1945, Germany was partitioned and occupied, with one-quarter of its territory forming the communist German Democratic Republic (GDR), which became part of the Soviet-dominated eastern European power bloc, and the remaining three-quarters being ruled by the liberal democratic Federal German Republic (FDR), which owed allegiance to the Western allies. The city of Berlin, located in the East German sector, was divided between the Western allies and the Soviet Union. The greatest symbol of the division of Germany was the 'Berlin Wall' erected by the communist East German regime in 1961.

From 1945 until the Berlin Wall came down in 1989, historians in the communist East and those in the democratic West adopted totally different approaches to analysing the Nazi period. During this era, non-German historians contributed more heavily to the historical debate on the Nazi phenomenon than had been the case for any other period of history. The study of Hitler and Nazism appeared to be as much a part of international history as of the national history of Germany. The Nazi phenomenon was an historical lesson that had universal interest and fascination. It was also a money-spinner for publishers, filmmakers and TV producers who quickly discovered that 'Hitler sells'. As a result, the historical debate spread around the world, which tended to make it difficult for any single historian to absorb the mass of material produced year by year.

In the 1950s, the interpretation of Adolf Hitler as primarily responsible for the 'German tragedy' was welcomed and endorsed by most West German historians. The two leading West German historians at the time, Gerhard Ritter and Friedrich Meinecke, representing the prevailing orthodoxy on the Nazi era, claimed Nazism was a unique phenomenon, a non-German sub-growth, which had planted itself in the otherwise healthy development of the German state. It had no parallel in German history. It was the will of a single madman. The most odious features of Nazism – extreme nationalism, anti-Semitism and social Darwinism – were all imported from outside Germany. Even Hitler's passionate desire to control eastern Europe, and his virulent anti-Semitism, owed more to his Austrian upbringing than his adopted home. Put this way, Nazism was depicted as a fatal derailment of recent German history from its pre-Nazi road to enlightenment and progress. For most West Germans, the idea of being bullied and held hostage for twelve years by an evil dictator who had destroyed their previous healthy historical development offered some comfort in a traumatic period. It also fitted in very nicely with the political desire of the US, French and British governments to support the rebuilding of democracy in Germany.

This complacent orthodoxy on the Nazi era by West German historians was not really challenged until the early 1960s, when the eminent German historian Fritz Fischer argued that Adolf Hitler was no ghost in the otherwise healthy German machine who had turned a healthy modern industrial society into a criminal and bestial dictatorship. On the contrary, Adolf Hitler was very much a 'German statesman' whose expansionist policies were similar to those of Bethmann Hollweg, the German Chancellor who launched the First World War. What is more, Fisher claimed that German foreign policy from 1871 to 1945 changed its form, but not its central aims. But it was Fischer's claim of a clear continuity in German history that aroused the greatest amount of criticism. Fisher argued that Hitler had gained power through an alliance between the traditional, agrarian, military and industrial elites who dominated German society and himself, the petit bourgeois leader of the Nazi Party. The 'old gang' who brought Hitler to power in January 1933 represented continuity with the leaders of pre-1914 Germany because they were contemptuous of Weimar democracy: just like the Nazis, they wanted the destruction of communism and the restoration of Germany as the dominant military power in Europe. Fisher suggested the formation of the alliance between the old guard and the Nazis in 1933 has to be understood as a reaction to the German defeat in the First World War. The anti-democratic and militaristic attitudes which were active in German military and industrial elites before 1914 remained operative during the Weimar era and became extremely powerful in the period leading up to the appointment of Hitler as German Chancellor. The elites that ruled Germany, and the Nazis, shared a common belief and objective: they did not accept the outcome of the First World War, and they desired European domination by Germany. It was only the amount of violence they were willing to deploy in the achievement of their aims that caused friction between Hitler and the old guard.

The 'Fisher controversy' raged for most of the 1960s and 1970s. Ritter, who became Fisher's leading German critic, refused to accept there was evidence of a unified German desire for war before 1914, or a plan for world domination, or genocide among the elites that ran Germany before 1914, and he suggested there were major differences between the Nazis and the old guard during the Nazi era. By the end of the 1970s, however, Fisher's two essential points, namely, that Germany was militaristic and desired European expansion many years before Hitler ever came to national prominence, and that there were important elements of continuity between the regimes of pre-1914 Germany and the Nazi era, particularly on foreign policy, were widely accepted. Just as the leaders of Wilhelmine Germany had believed Germany could become a superpower on a world scale before 1914, so Hitler and many of the leading members of the 'old gang' who appointed him German Chancellor believed much the same in 1933. The view that Hitler – at the time he came to power – represented a right-wing consensus in Germany could no longer be seriously dismissed.

What the heated 'Fisher debate' also achieved was to bring German historical work on the Nazi era into the broader international debate which had hitherto dictated the research agenda. The 'Fisher controversy' was a fundamental turning point in the post-war historical debate. It weakened the bland rigidity of West German debate on Nazism which had concentrated on high politics and foreign policy, while striving to avoid controversy. The debate over the 'Fisher thesis' was also important in rebuilding the credibility of German historical scholarship. Most importantly, a German historian had emerged at the centre of the international discussion on the Nazi phenomenon.

Fisher also prompted a more lengthy consideration among historians of a proposition originally put forward by Lewis Namier, namely, that Germany had followed a unique historical path to modernity (*Sonderweg*), which had contributed to Hitler's rise to power and the tragedy that followed. Ralf Dahrendorf showed in the 1960s that voting support for the Nazi Party grew in the early 1930s primarily because Germany had allowed a modern industrial economy to develop in a society where old semi-feudal elites had retained a dominant position and had allowed a political culture to develop that was anti-democratic and militaristic in outlook. It was, therefore, not the nature of modern German capitalism, which pitted right against left, that caused the growth in support for Nazism, but it was the pre-modern forces in German society that brought Hitler to power. The implication of this argument was that, if Germany had developed a strong middle class wedded to democracy before 1914, as occurred in many other stable Western industrial societies, then Nazism could never have prospered, especially among middle-class voters.

In the 1970s, many German historians used German archives extensively for the first time, and they started to challenge the view that Nazism grew out of a distorted German path towards modernity which had differed from other industrial nations. Most studies of German society from 1871 to 1914 tended to reveal that Germany had undergone a bourgeois revolution before 1914. Even the German army was incorporating members of the middle classes into its ranks before 1914. Yet in spite of these important qualifications, Fisher's central view of continuity in German foreign policy found wide acceptance. It could hardly be denied that the elite group that 'invited' Hitler into office in 1933 had done everything possible to undermine democracy for years beforehand, and had elevated the Nazi leader to high office in the hope that he would establish a popular authoritarian regime which they would control. However, the one area to which the continuity thesis cannot be applied is the unique racial ideas of the Nazi Party, which ultimately led to the extermination policies of Hitler's regime during the Second World War. Indeed, the racial element of Nazism does appear to weaken the idea of 'total' continuity, and emphasises that what Hitler wanted to achieve for his 'Third Reich' went far beyond what his alliance partners in 1933 ever envisaged when they brought him to power.

Not surprisingly, East German historians took little interest in the 'Fisher thesis' and interpreted the Nazi era very differently. Rejecting the view that history is about great individuals shaping historical change, East German historians stressed economic and social change as being the motive force of historical change. They rejected as simplistic the idea that the cataclysmic events in Germany during the Nazi era could be attributed to one wicked individual. East German historians, greatly influenced by Marxist theory, claimed they had made a clean break with the Nazi past, while their West German counterparts were trying to downplay their own complicity with the Nazi regime in order to revive capitalism in the West. A key part of this process, argued East German historians, was to peddle the fiction that all Germans were 'taking orders' from the criminal Nazi regime.

Most East German historians in the immediate post-war period tended to concentrate not on the criminality of the Nazi regime, but on the nature and role of fascism in Europe during the inter-war period and the broader economic crisis in the capitalist system. In most East German studies of the Nazi phenomenon Hitler was portrayed as the 'agent' and 'willing tool' of capitalist big business: the tank commander of the monopoly capitalists. His chosen mission, defined by his capitalist string pullers, was to destroy organised labour, shield the German economy from foreign competition, and find new sources of raw materials for German monopoly capitalists in eastern Europe through brutal wars of plunder. Of course, these subjective views were hardly original. In the 1920s, the Comintern had persistently linked capitalism with fascism. Drawing on Lenin's 1916 writings on the 'highest stage of capitalism', Marxist writers during the 1920s depicted fascism as a reactionary mass movement, whose chief aim was to destroy organised labour.

The rise of fascism was the final stage of bourgeois-capitalist rule. It was essentially elitist and backward-looking in outlook, and cruel and tyrannical in power. It was an organised capitalist rearguard action which used and abused the restricting and narrow emotion of patriotism to stoke up irrational and intolerant prejudice against people of different races and language, thereby hoping to halt the broader and progressive communist desire to truly transform society for the benefit of every member of it. Even the mass popularity of Hitler and Mussolini, claimed Marxist writers, was the product of media manipulation.

Even before the collapse of communism in eastern Europe during the late 1980s and its subsequent demise elsewhere, these impressionist left-wing views of Hitler and fascism were not taken very seriously outside the Soviet bloc, and were roundly dismissed by West German historians as self-serving left-wing rhetoric lacking in substance. Indeed, most of the detailed historical studies which have examined the supposed close link between 'big business' and the rise of Hitler have shown Nazism was the last – not the first – resort for German capitalists. Yet the discrediting of East German views within the historical debate should not lead to the simplistic counter-conclusion which suggests that German industrialists did not favour the end of democracy in Germany in 1933. Nor should we accept that capitalists opposed the weakening of organised labour that the Nazis promised. In fact, the Nazis in power provided a type of rule which benefited German capital-ists enormously. Even so, the capitalists did not pull the strings of either Hitler or the elites who brought him to power. A more sophisticated Marxist view of the circumstances surrounding the rise to power of Hitler and the Nazis, and one that has more credibility, argues that during a period of severe political crisis, such as existed in Germany during the 1930s, a party or leader who could restore the 'hegemony' of the ruling class would prove very attractive. Hence, the idea of a 'power cartel' in favour of maintaining the hegemony of a ruling elite over German society and eliminating some key opponents does have some credence in explaining how Hitler came to power.

As a counterweight to discussions concerning the nature of fascism being linked to a crisis in the capitalist system following the upheaval of the First World War, many West German historians looked to the concept of 'totalitarianism' to explain the European crisis between 1914 and 1945. It was claimed totalitarian states of the fascist and communist variety were very similar. Carl Friedrich outlined six central components of a totalitarian state:

1. an official ideology geared towards an historical goal, which is instilled into the entire population;
2. a single mass party led by a dominant individual;

3. a brutal secret police;
4. monopoly control of the media;
5. a monopoly over weapons;
6. coercion or central control of the economy.

The regimes of both Hitler and Stalin match most of the major aspects of the totalitarian concept, yet the term 'totalitarian' was seldom used by the Nazi leadership before 1933 and is more useful in analysing the Nazis in power.

A better way of examining the rise of Nazism is to view it as a unique revolution of the right, with clear goals of its own, which were not similar to the ideas of communism or to the policies of the traditional German right. Nazism, according to Mosse, was not an attempt to turn back the clock to a pre-industrial romanticised German past, nor a mere continuation of German militarism in another uniform, but instead offered a new and distinctive movement: a genuinely radical third way between liberal democracy and socialism. Indeed, Mosse suggests the unique characteristics of Nazism make it impossible to bracket it alongside other forms of totalitarianism or even other types of fascism. A great deal of recent research on the social basis of Nazi electoral support has shown that the dynamic aspects of the Nazi programme, especially its promise to modernise Germany for the benefit of the German people, attracted as many voters as the backward-looking and counter-revolutionary aspects of the Nazi electoral platform. What is more, Hitler's emphasis on gaining *Lebensraum* in eastern Europe promised to exploit agricultural resources using modern industrial techniques. The 'new Germany' promised by the Nazis involved strong industrial and agricultural sectors. Hitler promised new cities as well as new villages.

The growing interest in why voters were attracted to the Nazis before 1933 emerged during the 1970s and escalated during the 1980s through a plethora of local studies. There is scarcely a single German town which has not become the subject of a study of who voted for the Nazis in democratic elections before 1933. Most of these studies have tended to show that the Nazi Party, although supported primarily by a strong nucleus composed of members of the middle class and rural voters, also attracted electoral support from a much broader spectrum of voters than any other party in the Weimar period.

At the centre of the Western historical debate on the rise of Hitler and the Nazis, however, remains the position, role and significance of Adolf Hitler, who was underestimated for much of the period before he came to power, and who continues to be trivialised in many studies even today. There have been more biographies of Hitler than almost any other major historical figure. In addition, numerous 'psycho-histories' have focused on

'Hitler's mind', his sexuality, his childhood, and much else. The familiar face of the Nazi leader is never far from a TV screen, a web site, or a bookshop near you. People of all shades of political opinion are fascinated by the Nazi dictator, while, of course, except in the case of a small number of fanatics on the extreme right, always professing to despise everything he stood for. By and large, the Hitler phenomenon has taken on all the characteristics of a horrific accident: we want to walk past, but somehow, we have to stop and have a look.

Yet Hitler's contribution to the leadership, propaganda and ideology of Nazism is so important that to downplay his significance, or to view National Socialism as a mere sub-branch of a larger phenomenon called 'fascism', appears difficult to sustain. Of course, such a view must be qualified by stressing that the freedom of action of any individual, no matter how seemingly powerful, is always restrained by economic, social and political factors outside their control. The question of whether Hitler was the dynamic creator of events or a 'prisoner of circumstances' is difficult to resolve. Even so, Hitler was much more of a creator than a prisoner of events. He created the Nazi Party and moulded it into a major political force. National Socialism, although an amalgam of a number of influences, can be accurately called 'Hitlerism'. To believe German history would have taken the same course if Hitler had not existed is incorrect. Hitler was a politician who made a fundamental difference to the course of the events in which he participated. Indeed, it is now generally accepted that Hitler had a programme of action which was formulated in the years before he came to power. Even Klaus Hildebrand, who rejects the idea that the Nazi phenomenon can be reduced solely to Hitler, does concede that the 'Hitler factor' was central to the development of the Nazi Party, its rise to power and the policies of the Third Reich.

In more recent times, there has also been an important debate about how the Nazi era should now be analysed. If Nazism was a unique phenomenon, not linked to the German past, then it can remain in a special place, separated from the rest of German history. In the mid-1980s a number of German historians suggested it was time for the Nazi era to be treated in the same objective manner as any other period of history. Martin Broszat claimed the evil of Hitler and the Nazis had been replayed so often it had lost much of its ability to shock new generations. Accordingly, Broszat suggested the moral condemnation which formed a vital part of most studies of Nazism in the immediate post-war period should now be replaced by a more objective analysis. However, the attempt by German historians to 'normalise' the Nazi era, which was a legitimate protest against much of the moralising history that had been written by non-German historians on that era, was fiercely resisted, especially outside Germany, and particularly among Jewish historians concerned about what effect such a 'normalisation' might have on the historical debate on Nazi racial theories and policies. Saul Friedlander argued that if the Nazi era was like any other historical period then Hitler's 'war against the Jews' would soon be viewed as just another example of 'genocide' or 'ethnic cleansing'. There was also a quite natural worry expressed within the public debate that normalising life in the Nazi era, even for the purposes of invigorating scholarly academic research, could lead to Nazism being seen as attractive by younger members of society. Fears were even expressed by some German politicians of the possibility of the development of a 'Hitler cult' in Germany if study of Nazi Germany became 'normalised'. What the heated 'historians' debate' showed was that the historical debate on Nazi Germany was still wedded to prevailing political and international pressures. It revealed too that Nazi Germany still belonged to world history, not merely to German history. Yet the limitations imposed on the study of the Nazi phenomenon by the prevailing international climate of political opinion had already tended to lead to increasingly sterile and predictable history studies of Hitler and Nazism, which had done little to deepen understanding.

Today, the 'historians' debate' of the mid-1980s appears a very reasonable request. Ever since that time a great deal of change has occurred both inside and outside Germany. To begin with, Germany is no longer divided into the democratic West and the communist East. The Cold War between the democratic West and the communist Eastern bloc has also ended. As a result, we have seen the complete collapse of Marxist East German and Soviet studies of the Nazi era.

Not surprisingly, these cataclysmic events have had an astonishing impact on the historical debate. A far greater interest in why Hitler rose to power has emerged than ever before. There has also been a fresh attempt to examine the continuities in German history. These new, post-1989 studies have also tended to locate Nazism in a much broader international context than ever before. The fall of the Berlin Wall in 1989 also put an end to the so-called 'special German path' debate. Hitler's legacy was not the permanent division of Germany. Much recent historical work on Nazi Germany has been free of the previous moral framework, which often suffocated it. Indeed, most of the best new work on the Nazi era now comes from German scholars who are willing to face up to the past with open minds.

Another key aspect of the post-Cold War debate on Hitler and Nazism has been the willingness of historians to examine Nazi ideology more closely, and to take it far more seriously in the context of the time in which it proved popular. In recent studies on Hitler it has been stressed that Nazism was not as backward looking as was previously supposed. On the contrary, Hitler's ultimate goal was an advanced industrial and technologically modern Germany.

There is also a greater concentration in the recent debate on the influence and centrality of communism to the rise of Nazism. The idea of Nazism as a reaction by certain groups in German society to the growth of communism, which was argued by communist writers in the 1920s, is now seen as a much more important factor to the growth of Nazism than was previously argued in the Cold War era. It is becoming increasingly clear that the Nazi Party was engaged in a civil war against communism throughout Germany, and, later, in eastern Europe. The bitter ideological clash between Nazism and communism in the early part of the twentieth century is now viewed as central to understanding the rise and fall of the Nazi Party. It seems the rest of the world was dragged into this life and death struggle.

What has not emerged since the fall of the Berlin Wall is the development of a Hitler cult in Germany. On the contrary, the objective approach of German historians to their own past is making it possible to see more clearly why ordinary Germans in their millions were seduced by Hitler's charismatic power.

The most high-profile controversy within the historical debate over Hitler and Nazism in recent years was ignited in the late 1990s by Daniel Goldhagen, a Jewish political scientist based in the USA, who claimed the Holocaust was not a secret and clandestine enterprise, carried out on the orders of Hitler, but was the inevitable consequence of long-standing anti-Semitic attitudes ingrained in German society. Even more startling was Goldhagen's claim that those who carried out the order to eliminate the Jews were 'ordinary' Germans who were 'willing executioners'. Instead of hiding behind the post-war myth that they were 'taking orders' from the criminally barbaric Nazi regime, Goldhagen controversially suggested that Germans must carry the collective guilt for the Holocaust. The 'Goldhagen controversy' created a political sensation in Germany, and made headline news around the world. It opened up once more the troubled relationship between modern Germany and its Nazi past. Goldhagen's book, although it provided a simplistic view as to why the Holocaust occurred, did raise the possibility that it was anti-Semitism that explained Hitler's popularity within Germany before and after 1933. Yet close examination of the pre-1933 period shows that anti-Semitism, though a central aspect of Nazi ideology, was not the major issue highlighted by the Nazis in their election campaigns. It is probably worth adding that local election studies of Nazi voters show that anti-Semitism turned off more 'ordinary' German electors than it attracted.

The 'Goldhagen controversy' threatened to return the debate on Nazi Germany to the bitterness that characterised the pre-1989 era. However, this has not happened. On the contrary, many of the older historical debates on Hitler and Nazism have either lost energy or simply run out of steam. The various attempts in the 1960s and 1970s, largely prompted by Marxist historians, to find a general theory of fascism have literally withered away, helped along by the general decline in the popularity and relevance of Marxism in Europe and elsewhere. The previous fascination with examining the role of the 'working class' in Weimar and Nazi Germany has also faded, as the importance of the organised working class in modern developed countries has also declined as a political force. Even the once heated debate over the aims of Hitler's foreign policy now appears very tired, and unlikely to produce any new startling or thought-provoking work in the future. The question of the relationship between the Nazis and big business has also been resolved. It is now accepted that Hitler was not a puppet of big business in the years before he came to office. However, the close relationship between Hitler and big business after he came to power is now being more extensively examined by business historians who have recently produced important new studies on Nazi influence in companies such as I. G. Farben, Volkswagen and Daimler-Benz.

Perhaps the most important aspect of the post-1989 historical research output on the Nazi phenomenon is that most of the best and more enlightening new work on the Holocaust is being produced by German historians. What has not changed in the current debate is the centrality of Hitler to the rise and fall of Nazism. On the contrary, Hitler's importance to the Nazi phenomenon has been significantly enhanced in recent studies, and the general public still buys new biographies on the Nazi dictator in greater numbers than ever before.

Indeed, something fundamental has occurred: the debate over Nazi Germany now resembles 'normal' historical debate in a way it never did before 1989. The former bitterness has disappeared, to be replaced by genuine disagreements over interpretation. This is not to say that historians find it easy to remove their own moral – and natural – detestation of the worst aspects of Nazism from their writings, but merely to point out that routine moralising has been replaced by genuine analysis. The current debate on Nazi Germany is far more interesting as a consequence. Looking at the past through a moral framework always produces bad history.

At the same time as the historical debate is probing questions in more depth, however, the 'Hitler industry' grows daily, fuelled by an endless diet of TV programmes debating every aspect of Hitler's private life. There are also far too many books produced which unashamedly attempt to appeal to the mass market and end up trivialising the Nazi era. The 'Hitler industry' has now extended to the Internet, with equally worrying consequences.

Nevertheless, it still remains extremely important to examine how a democratic country can turn into a dictatorship, and to explain why Hitler became the most popular politician in Germany because of votes recorded in democratic elections. In understanding why Hitler rose to power we are really looking at what can happen in a democracy if people are not willing to defend its fundamental principles. In the period when the Nazis rose to power, very few German people could have predicted what Nazism would come to represent, and if they had known, it is difficult to accept that so many millions of people would have voted for the Nazi Party in the first place.

By recognising why Hitler was so popular with so many millions of ordinary German people before and after 1933 we are getting closer to the importance of Nazism as a popular phenomenon in its particular place and time. Indeed, by understanding why Hitler was so popular with large sections of German society, especially among the normally stable middle classes, we can appreciate more fully that it is possible for such a nightmare to happen again in a different form.

It is, of course, equally possible that Hitler was a product of a particular place and time, the circumstances of which may never be repeated. The economic and political upheaval in Germany from 1930 to 1933 did provide fertile ground for a would-be demagogue who promised strong leadership to a country decimated by defeat and economic upheaval. At that time, Hitler's utopian vision of a new Germany proved attractive. Hitler's unique personal contribution was to manipulate the power brokers and millions of voters to accept that he was the 'last hope for Germany'. He played on the fear that, if he did not come to power, a communist revolution would be the inevitable consequence. He also persuaded the army that his foreign policy goals, especially rearmament, would benefit them. He promised a new deal for farmers, skilled workers and for the middle classes. He claimed two groups, the socialists and the Jews, were at the root of all Germany's problems. The liberals who supported democracy were branded by Hitler as the agents of these groups. It was clear the Nazis would deal with the 'socialist menace' ruthlessly, but few voters imagined Hitler's anti-Semitism would result in the organised murder arranged by the German government during the Second World War.

After Hitler was released from prison in December 1924 for his part in the attempted overthrow of the Bavarian government in November 1923, he set out to build up a national party organisation that would give the Nazis a broader base and efficient local organisation. At the same time, he established his own dominance over the Nazi Party to a point where his leadership was unchallenged.

Once the depression hit Germany, Hitler's careful construction of an efficient party machine allied to effective propaganda and his own charismatic leadership started to pay off. To believe it was simply the economic circumstances of the early 1930s which enabled a gross mediocrity to rise to national prominence is an absurd hypothesis, just as it is to suggest German democracy was simply destroyed in a series of catastrophic errors by those who controlled its political power centre. Hitler very skilfully played on fears brought about by the economic depression, and planted fear in the minds of those still in work that they would lose their jobs if they did not help to put the Nazis in power. In a country where national feelings ran deep, Hitler's promise to right the wrongs of Versailles, to drag Germany out of depression, to deal with the communist threat, to put people back to work and, above all, to create social harmony and to restore Germany to national greatness struck a chord with many millions of German voters.

This powerful Nazi brew, distilled by Hitler over many years, proved intoxicating to many Germans. Most of these supporters came from the middle classes and the peasantry, but as Hitler's popularity grew they came to include some members of the working classes and the upper middle classes. The Nazis were supported in all classes by a large proportion of young people, who seem to have been attracted by Hitler's utopian view that 'tomorrow' belonged to them.

Although the Nazis never won an overall majority of Germans to this vision, they did win over 13 million voters in democratic elections to their essentially classless appeal by 1932, and they could be sure of much more support if Hitler's promises were carried out in power. The Nazi stress on the need for self-sacrifice, for putting the nation before class, struck a chord with many voters who opposed the development of class-based politics in German society and longed for strong leadership and social harmony to be restored.

In recent studies of the Nazi appeal to voters before 1933, it has been shown how important Hitler's promise to create a popular folk community (*Volksgemeinschaft*) was in attracting new voters. It is this emphasis, rather than anti-Semitism, or outrage against the Treaty of Versailles, that explains the broad appeal of the Nazis in democratic elections before 1933. The concept of *Volksgemeinschaft* was an inclusive and integrationist concept for Germans, and it was the most utopian and positive aspect of the Nazi electoral platform. It was linked to an ideal of national identity. It also allowed the Nazis to suggest they could create a new type of social harmony and national solidarity. The idea of *Volksgemeinschaft* was also a concept of citizenship in a modern society. At a time of economic upheaval this idea of social harmony was extremely important in the growth of support for the Nazi Party.

There is little doubt that the rise of the Nazis was connected to a particular set of circumstances, many of which, though present elsewhere in Europe, were more accentuated in Germany, which did not have a strong democratic tradition. Nevertheless, we must remember that all the problems that destabilised Germany after 1918 were not present simultaneously. Germany was politically and economically unstable from 1919 to 1923, but democracy survived intact. German democracy collapsed during the early 1930s. Hence, the timing of the fall of the Weimar Republic is crucial for understanding why Hitler came to power. It seems the second deep economic crisis in Germany after 1929 did galvanise those on the right of German politics to seek an authoritarian solution to divisions in politics and society.

Adolf Hitler was passionately committed to destroying Weimar democracy, and the growth of support for the Nazi Party from 1930 onwards destabilised democracy more than any other single factor, because it brought the Nazi Party to the forefront of German politics and weakened those parties committed to upholding democracy. President Hindenburg, who was old and frail, appointed a series of unpopular and faceless right-wing politicians between 1930 and 1932, without any popular support. When Hindenburg appointed Hitler as German Chancellor in 1933, he had already tried all other right-wing alternatives. At the time Hitler came to power he was the most popular and charismatic right-wing politician in Germany, enjoying the support of the great majority of voters on the centre right.

Accordingly, this study argues that it was Adolf Hitler's charismatic leadership of the Nazi Party, supported by efficient organisation and effective propaganda, that gave the right-wing conservative elements of German society what they longed for: a party that would champion nationalist interests and create an authoritarian regime that would restore their position in German society. To believe – as some historians do – that Hitler's appeal to a large section of the German people would simply have melted away, and the Nazi Party been consigned to a rapidly declining role in Germany, does not fit the facts. Once Adolf Hitler reached the main-stream of German politics, democracy was doomed, and a Hitler-led government was inevitable.

The analysis that follows is structured in the following way. In Part Two, the early life of Adolf Hitler and the growth of the Nazi Party from 1918 to 1924 are examined in some detail. In further chapters, Nazi ideology, organisation, membership and propaganda tactics are analysed. In Chapter 6, there is a detailed examination of Hitler's rise to power in the crucial period from 1925 to 1933. In Part Three, there is a critical assessment of why Hitler came to power. The book also contains a set of documents, a glossary of key terms, a Who's Who of leading characters, and a bibliographical essay, which gives advice on further reading.

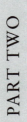

PART TWO   ANALYSIS

CHAPTER TWO

ADOLF HITLER: PERSONALITY AND EARLY LIFE

Adolf Hitler is the most recognisable historical figure of the twentieth century. No one else has aroused so much historical controversy, or given rise to such morbid popular fascination. It is, indeed, impossible to conceive of German history – and world history – taking the same course if Adolf Hitler had never lived. Yet the available evidence for Hitler's early life is extremely fragmented. Hitler's own account, offered in his book *Mein Kampf*, is largely inaccurate, while the very few people who knew him in the formative years of his life offered their evidence many years later, which no doubt coloured their judgement.

FAMILY BACKGROUND

Adolf Hitler, who was baptised as a Catholic, was born at 6.30 p.m. on 20 April 1889 at the Gasthof zum Pommer, in the Austrian town of Braunau am Inn, close to the Austro-German frontier. Hitler was the fourth child of the union between Alois Hitler and Klara Poelzl. Their first three children – Gustav, Ida and Otto – all died before any of them had reached the age of three. Two more children were born after Adolf: Edmund (born in 1894, but died in 1900) and Paula, born in 1896, who lived into old age. The survival of only two children out of a family of six was by no means abnormal in the context of the times.

Alois Hitler, Hitler's father, was born on 27 June 1837, in the small village of Strones. He was actually christened Alois Schicklgruber, and was the only son of Maria Anna Schicklgruber, the daughter of Johann Schicklgruber. The family were peasants, who had farmed land for several generations in the Waldviertal, a hilly and wooded region in the lower north-west of Austria, on the border of Bohemia. At the time of his birth, Alois Hitler was termed an 'illegitimate child' because the space allotted to the father on the birth register was left blank.

A great deal of historical speculation, much of it idle and fanciful, has been spent attempting to explain who Adolf Hitler's grandfather really was.

Hitler always avoided discussing the subject, as he feared there might be some Jewish blood in his veins. The true facts remain somewhat cloudy to this day. In 1842, Maria Schicklgruber married Johann Georg Hiedler (often spelt 'Hitler' or 'Huttler' in the area), a 50-year-old miller whose family came from Spital, located about 15 miles outside Strones. It is often assumed – quite plausibly – that Maria (who died in 1847) finally wed Johann Georg Hiedler because he was the real father of Alois. But this has never been conclusively proven. From the time of his mother's death, or perhaps even before, Alois went to live with Johann Nepomuk Hiedler, his father's brother (who effectively became his stepfather). Even so – in 1876 – Alois registered Johann George Hiedler (who had died nineteen years earlier) as his father, but in the birth register 'Hiedler' is spelt 'Hitler' (meaning 'smallholder'). From 1 January 1877, Alois could legally use the surname Hitler under Austrian law. This decision ensured that the future Nazi leader was not called Adolf Schicklgruber. Thousands of Germans passionately shouting 'Heil Schicklgruber' just does not sound right.

The reason for the belated change of name by Alois from Schicklgruber to Hitler has provoked much speculation among historians. One theory suggests Nepomuk wanted the name change in order to preserve the hereditary continuance of the Hiedler name, and possibly offered Alois a legacy as an inducement to change his name. A second – less plausible – theory claims Nepomuk was the 'real' father of Alois all along, which could explain why Alois went to live with him shortly after his mother's death. A third – also less plausible – theory puts forward the view that neither Georg nor Nepomuk Hiedler was the father of Alois: his real father was really a Jew called Frankenberger who lived in the small Austrian village of Graz. Adolf Hitler was concerned enough about this latter possibility to ask Hans Frank, a leading Nazi, to investigate the matter during the 1930s. In a confidential report, Frank concluded that Maria Schicklgruber gave birth to Alois while she worked as a cook in the house of a Jewish family called Frankenberger in Graz. The report also made the astonishing claim that Frankenberger paid maintenance for the child to Maria Schicklgruber. If this is true, then the 'Final Solution' of the 'Jewish Question' was actually ordered by someone who had Jewish blood in his veins. However, the claims in the report of Hans Frank have subsequently been shown to be untrue. To begin with, no family called Frankenberger ever lived in Graz during the 1830s, according to surviving records. There is also no evidence showing Maria Schicklgruber ever living or working in Graz, and no evidence of maintenance payments being paid to her. In the final analysis, the most plausible theory is the straightforward one: Johann Georg Hiedler was the real father of Alois. It seems his brother Nepomuk wanted this acknowledged legally before he died. Of course, there is a possibility that Nepomuk was the real father, which may help to explain why Alois lived with him for most of his life. But, if this was so, why did Alois not register Nepomuk as his real father when he had the opportunity? The answer must be that he knew all along that Georg Hiedler was his father.

PARENTS

In *Mein Kampf*, Hitler portrayed his father as a lowly customs official, who brought up his family in a state of near poverty. This was definitely untrue. Hitler's father carved out a very successful career as a well-paid and highly respected customs official. From 1855 to 1895, Alois Hitler worked as a customs officer in several towns in Austria. He was quite frequently promoted, wore the grand uniform of a leading Hapsburg official, lived in affluent circumstances and enjoyed a salary and a public status on a par with the headmaster of a private secondary school.

The private life of Alois Hitler was quite colourful – for a customs officer. In 1864 he married Anna Glass, who was fourteen years his senior, relatively well off, but in failing health. In effect, Alois was what the tabloids today would call a toy boy. The marriage, which produced no children, was not a success, and in 1880 the couple were granted a legal separation. By this time, Alois was already in the middle of another torrid love affair, with Franziska (Fanny) Matzelberger, a very youthful maid. The couple had a son, Alois (born in 1882), and shortly after Anna Glass died (in 1883) Alois married Franziska. Only a few weeks after the wedding, Franziska gave birth to a daughter, Angela. In August 1884, however, Franziska died of tuberculosis, aged only 23. Alois was not particularly overcome with grief about the untimely death of his young wife. In fact, while Fanny was seriously ill, Alois had started a love affair with Klara Poelzl, his second cousin, and the granddaughter of Nepomuk Hiedler. On 7 January 1885 Alois Hitler, now aged 47, married Klara, then aged just 24. Klara was pregnant on her wedding day and, given their close family relationship, the couple needed a special dispensation from the Vatican for their marriage to go ahead. Indeed, for many years after the marriage Klara continued to address Alois as 'uncle'.

CHILDHOOD

Although he moved home frequently, Alois Hitler always provided his family with a comfortable lifestyle. Adolf Hitler was no 'child of poverty', as he later claimed in *Mein Kampf*. He was a clean, well-dressed, middle-class boy who lived in affluent surroundings and attended fee-paying schools. At home there were handmade curtains on the windows, carpets on the floor, and fruit, vegetables, and a bee hive, producing honey, in the garden. The Hitler household often included a cook and a maidservant. In Branau am Inn (where the family lived from 1889 to 1892), they had a large house with a picturesque garden. In Passau, Bavaria, from 1892 to 1895, the family home was a large apartment. From 1895 to 1897, they resided in a large country house in Hafeld, occupying nine acres of land, which had been bought from a minor Austrian nobleman. Between 1897 and 1898, the family lived in another palatial apartment in the small rural town of Lambach. In November 1898, Alois moved to another pleasant house with a large garden in Leonding, a village on the outskirts of Linz, where he was to remain for the rest of his life. Of all the different places Adolf Hitler lived during his childhood, he always regarded the home near Linz as his favourite.

All the constant moving around that was a feature of Hitler's childhood meant he changed schools often, and mixed with a new and unfamiliar set of schoolmates. Adolf Hitler was a lively and able pupil whose academic abilities were greatly hampered by his lifelong dislike of hard work. At his first primary (elementary) school, at Fischlam, near Lambach (where he started on 1 May 1895), he was very popular ('a little ringleader') with his schoolmates. At this time, he found school work 'ridiculously easy', leaving him 'with so much free time that the sun saw more of me than my room' (Kershaw, 1998:15). He gained good marks in all his academic subjects, and he became an enthusiastic member of the school choir and a regular churchgoer. At his next school, in Lambach, he continued to achieve good marks. At the third elementary school he attended – in Leonding – he also performed well in his first year there, but during his final year he became introspective, sullen, moody, obstinate, and more inclined than before to go his own way. With such a generally lazy and uninterested attitude to school work, his marks slipped to 'below average'. One possible reason for the sudden downturn in his mood – and his marks – during his final year at primary school may have been the sudden death (due to measles) of his younger brother, Edmund.

Outside school, the young Hitler was no different from any boy of his age during this period. He enjoyed playing imaginary war games, and reading adventure stories in comics. He often led his schoolmates in rough and tumble games of cowboys and 'red Indians'. In such games, young Adolf always chose to play a red Indian (the underdog). His love of playing cowboys and Indians was inspired by reading the popular Wild West adventure stories of Karl May, a German writer who had never even visited America. Even after Hitler became German Chancellor he was still an avid reader of May's Western stories. Another of Hitler's passions as a youngster was playing war games. One of Hitler's favourites was to re-enact, with his friends, the Boer struggle against the British Empire. Hitler once more was on the side of the underdogs, this time the Boers, the plucky and obstinate South African farmers who defied the 'mighty British Empire' between 1899 and 1902.

It would be wrong, however, to depict Hitler's childhood as completely secure and tension free. The major source of Hitler's personal discontent as a child, notwithstanding the obvious negative psychological impact of the family's numerous house moves and the death of other close family members, was his difficult relationship with his father. Alois Hitler was strict, frugal, humourless and extremely domineering. He was also a heavy drinker, even though his drinking never interfered with his ability to do his job. Alois demanded 'absolute obedience' at home, and he frequently punished bad behaviour with physical punishment. Hitler later recalled: 'I never loved my father. I therefore feared him all the more. He had a terrible temper and often whipped me' (Waite, 1977: 137). Hitler later described his relationship with his father as a battle of competing wills. His father wanted him to become a senior civil servant, but his headstrong young son was equally determined to become a great artist. From his father, Hitler did not receive love and guidance, only stern and domineering orders, often issued under the threat of violence, and severely punished by violence when they were not obeyed. It is, of course, quite possible that Hitler's later passion for absolute dominance, his love of terror, can be attributed to the influence of his stern and domineering father.

If Adolf Hitler's father was a negative source of anger, his mother was definitely a compensatory positive source of love and affection in his life. Klara Hitler was a simple, quiet, uncomplicated, submissive and kind woman. Adolf Hitler had a very strong attachment to her. She watched over him as a child, pampered him and, whenever his father was not around, let him do what he liked. In *Mein Kampf* Hitler wrote: 'I honoured my father, but I loved my mother' (Kershaw, 1998: 12). Dr Bloch, the Hitler family doctor, claimed he had 'never witnessed a closer attachment' than the one between Adolf Hitler and his mother. No other woman ever compared to his mother. He carried a picture of her in his wallet all his life. As leader of Germany, he turned his mother's birthday into a national holiday.

Adolf Hitler often referred to 'being in love' with his mother, and mostly spoke of 'not liking' his father. In most 'normal' families, there is often a conflict between a child and one or other of its parents at various times, yet, many psychiatrists believe children are more likely to avoid mental health problems in later life if they love both parents in roughly equal proportions. This clearly did not happen in the case of Adolf Hitler. It has been suggested he had a dysfunctional relationship with both his parents. He may even have suffered (claim some psychologists) from an Oedipus complex, a theory first propounded by Sigmund Freud, which holds that, when rivalry with a parent of the same sex is never resolved, and when deep love feelings towards the parent of the opposite sex are not transferred to a sexual partner outside the family, then such a person is very likely to encounter mental problems in later life. The theory has some credence when applied to

Hitler, as he never did achieve a balanced relationship with both his parents, and he had few successful relationships with members of the opposite sex in later life. But whether Hitler was suffering from an Oedipus complex is psychological guesswork, based on extremely limited evidence. In any case, most of those who have been diagnosed as suffering in such a way do not go on to become murderous dictators. Nor do the family circumstances of all dictators fit the theory. In fact, if we did not know what was to come, we would surely conclude that Hitler's early childhood, in spite of some minor and unexceptional signs of emotional instability, was very ordinary, free of deprivation, and could not remotely be described as being at the extreme end of dysfunctional. As a result, writing off Hitler as a madman, though perhaps comforting, is a complete distortion of what he was really like.

YOUTH

On 17 September 1900, at the age of eleven, Adolf Hitler began his secondary education at the fee-paying *Realschule* in Linz. The transition from primary to secondary education proved difficult, and he was extremely negative towards his educational experience from beginning to end. The journey from Leonding to school involved a three-mile walk, which took over an hour to complete.

In the small town of Leonding, Adolf Hitler, the son of a respected local civil servant, enjoyed a high status among his fellow pupils. But in Linz, a larger town, with a population of 60,000 inhabitants, his fellow classmates, mostly composed of the sons of academics, businessmen, lawyers, doctors, and people of that kind, viewed him as a rough-hewn rustic. This may help to explain why he never made any close friends at the school. It was at his secondary school that he developed, for the first time, the alienating feeling of being an 'outsider', especially among his upper-middle-class contemporaries. At the *Realschule*, Hitler's marks fluctuated between 'average' and 'mediocre'. His teachers viewed the young Hitler as a boy certainly not lacking in talent, but as a moody, rather lazy pupil with a very stubborn streak. In *Mein Kampf*, Hitler claimed he took a minimal interest in most academic subjects except history, geography and art; his teacher (Dr Leonard Poetsch) fired his imagination – and his growing patriotism – with vivid stories of German nationalism; he loved reading maps and free-hand drawing. Hitler claimed he became a strongly emotional and passionate German nationalist during his time at secondary school. His favourite German heroes were the soldier-king Frederick the Great and Otto von Bismarck, the first German Chancellor. His poor performance at school was an act of defiance, or so he said, against his father's wish for him to become a civil servant when all he wanted to do was to become an artist.

On 3 January 1903, Alois Hitler collapsed and died after suffering a lung haemorrhage while drinking red wine in a local tavern. He was buried in Leonding cemetery two days later. The death of his father, although no doubt inwardly traumatic for a young teenager to cope with, appears to have come as something of a relief to Adolf, who was now free of his father's tyranny, and able to contemplate his own dream of becoming a great artist. With his father out of the picture, and with a doting mother who was willing to indulge his whims, the teenage Adolf neglected his school work like never before. He had to pass re-sit examinations in each of his remaining years at school. The headmaster of the *Realschule* at Linz, tired of his obvious indifference to school work, forced him to move to another *Realschule* at Steyr, some 25 miles away. In September 1905, Adolf Hitler passed his final re-sit examination in geometry. This made him eligible to gain the coveted school diploma (*Abitur*) after a further two years of study at a higher school, the *Oberrealschule*. He was not prepared to face any more schooling, and in the autumn of 1905 he persuaded his mother to let him leave, aged sixteen, without any qualifications. Hitler's self-inflicted failure at secondary school left him with a bitter and lifelong contempt for book-learned academics and intellectuals.

Over the next two years, Adolf Hitler became an expert in the art of loafing around. In June 1905, Klara Hitler sold the house in Leonding, and moved into a comfortable apartment in the Linz suburbs. At this stage in his life, Adolf Hitler resembled a Bohemian dilettante, with fairly long hair, a moustache, fashionable clothes and a dark hat. He was always seen outside carrying a black cane with a stylish ivory handle. He looked more like a budding Oscar Wilde than a future rabble-rousing dictator. He stayed up reading late into the night (usually books on German history, mythology and Western novels), and he never got up until sometime after noon. During the day he visited local cafés, art galleries and libraries. In the evening he often attended the local opera house (he particularly loved Wagner) with August Kubizek, a gifted young musician and the son of an upholsterer, who became his closest teenage friend.

The recollections of August Kubizek (or 'Gustl', as Hitler called him) are the major source for Hitler's life at this time. Kubizek's account of his friendship with Hitler was not published until 1954, and his views are somewhat clouded by his obvious admiration for the Nazi dictator. Even so, most historians believe that Kubizek's account, in spite of its obvious deficiencies, does contain important insights into the personality of Adolf Hitler at this formative stage of his life. Hitler met Kubizek at the opera house in Linz in the autumn of 1905. The relationship between these two teenagers consisted of Adolf doing most of the talking, and 'Gustl' taking the minor listening role. Hitler is described by Kubizek as 'high strung', with a tendency to 'fly off the handle' whenever conversation turned to discussions of the merits of schoolteachers, civil servants and local taxation. Kubizek did not notice

Hitler holding strong anti-Semitic views or being deeply interested in politics or foreign affairs. He does mention that Hitler once came out of a performance of *Rienzi*, an opera by Wagner, in 1906 claiming he would one day receive a 'mandate from the people' imploring him to lead them to 'the heights of freedom', but this sounds like Kubizek projecting onto the teenage Hitler his later political ambitions (Kubizek, 1954: 61). Hitler's greatest passions at this time were music, art and architecture. He scorned the idea of looking for a mundane job, dreaming instead of a career in the art world. To further this ambition, Hitler told 'Gustl' of his plan to try and gain entry to the illustrious Vienna Academy of Art. His determination to pursue an artistic career was strengthened further after a pleasurable holiday in the Austrian capital in May 1906. There were, however, no girlfriends in the life of these two teenage boys. Kubizek does mention Hitler's 'infatuation' with a young upper-class girl called Stephanie, whom he had seen in Linz town centre from time to time. But Hitler admired Stephanie from afar: he wrote several love poems about her, but they were never delivered. In fact, he never even spoke to her.

THE DEATH OF HITLER'S MOTHER

The most traumatic personal event of Hitler's youth was undoubtedly the death of his beloved mother. In January 1907, Klara Hitler became seriously ill with breast cancer, and underwent a life-saving mastectomy. In the summer of 1907, with his mother still recovering from her very serious operation, Hitler persuaded her to let him go to Vienna to sit the entrance examination for the Academy of Fine Arts. For a school drop-out who had spent the previous two years in idle bliss, this was an overly ambitious plan. He rented a small flat in Vienna, sat his entrance exam in October 1907, but failed. He described the examiners as 'fossilized Bureaucrats devoid of any understanding of young talent' (Hitler, 1936: 20). But his examiners were right: Hitler was an artist with a talent deficit. His paintings and drawings from this period show technical competence in copying other people's works, but no aptitude for creating original works of his own. Hitler could paint and draw buildings and landscapes, but not people. Art experts who have examined Hitler's work in detail suggest it lacks originality, but does not reveal a personality suffering from deep psychological difficulties. Even Hitler's tendency to paint buildings rather than portraits is viewed by psychologists as the product of an introverted personality, without any deep mental difficulties.

In the meantime, the health of Hitler's mother deteriorated rapidly. In late October 1907, Hitler returned to Linz to nurse her, night and day, during the worst period of her illness. On the evening of 21 December 1907, Klara Hitler died, with Hitler loyally at her bedside to the last beat of her heart. Dr Bloch, the Jewish family doctor who had given her close medical attention throughout her illness, later commented: 'In all my career I have never seen anyone as prostrate with grief as Adolf Hitler' (Shirer, 1961: 43). The death of his mother was a dreadful blow to Hitler, as he had lost the one person he ever felt any deep affection for.

At the tender age of eighteen, Hitler had no parents and lacked emotional and financial security. In *Mein Kampf*, Hitler claimed his mother's death led him to face – for the first time – the hitherto neglected problem of 'somehow making my own living' (Kershaw, 1998: 25). In reality, his financial position was not as impoverished as he later claimed. Hitler shared an inheritance from his mother of 2000 Kronen with his sister Paula. He also received an orphan's pension of 240 Kronen per annum. In addition, he had some money left from a 924-Kronen gift from his Aunt Johanna, part of which he used to fund his first Vienna trip. Hitler was not in a comfortable financial position after his mother died, but he was better off than the average student or manual labourer, and had no need to look for a job – at least for the time being.

THE VIENNA PERIOD, 1908–13

In February 1908, Hitler returned to Vienna, where he was to remain for the next five and a half years. Vienna was one of the great cosmopolitan capitals of Europe at the time: an ethnic melting pot of Germans, Czechs, Poles, Slovaks, Serbs, Croats, Italians, Rumanians and Hungarians. It contained the largest Jewish population of any German or Austrian city. In 1910, for example, 175,318 Jews resided in Vienna, making up 8.6 per cent of the population of the metropolis. Jewish people were prominent in academia, the legal and medical professions, finance, the mass media and the arts. There was also an underclass of poor eastern European Jews who lived in the run-down and poverty-ridden parts of the old city.

Hitler found life in cosmopolitan, sophisticated and ethnically diverse Vienna much harder to cope with than small-town Linz, especially when he ran short of money [*Doc. 1*]. In March 1908, he was joined in the capital by his close friend 'Gustl' Kubizek, who began his studies in music at the prestigious Vienna Academy of Music. For the next few months, these two close friends from Linz shared a flat together. In this period, Kubizek saw Hitler writing poetry, sketching the outline of a play – based on German mythology – and writing a derivative Wagner-style opera (which he never completed) (Kubizek, 1954: 213). Hitler continued to visit the opera regularly and, true to form, went to bed late at night and rose late in the morning. In other words, Hitler transferred his life of blissful idleness from Linz to Vienna.

In the summer of 1908, Kubizek returned to Linz for the summer vacation. In September, Hitler took the entrance exam at the Vienna Academy of Arts for a second time – and failed again. He was a certainty for failure, as he had not prepared for the exam, nor had he sought any advice from the Academy about how to improve his chances in the year since his first abject failure. Even so, this one was a shattering blow. It ended Hitler's teenage – and unrealistic – dream of becoming a 'great artist'. He slumped henceforth into a state of deep depression. In November 1908, Kubizek returned from Linz, but he found that Hitler had left the flat they shared, leaving no forwarding address.

Hitler was now alone, dependent on his own willpower. He later described his Vienna period as 'the saddest years of my life'. Yet this period of Hitler's early life, which has aroused much speculation among historians, is largely closed off to detailed historical research because of a severe lack of reliable sources. Hitler's own account of his Vienna years in *Mein Kampf* is unreliable, lacks all detail about his personal life, and attempts to portray his life as one long struggle against deprivation and poverty. Only a handful of people actually knew Hitler during this period, and even those who did know him recorded their views of him much later, thus distorting any understanding of what he was really like at the time.

Hitler's rejection by the Vienna art establishment was a great blow to his self-esteem, and it made him very bitter, as well as depressed. He had desperately wanted – although he later tried to deny it – to be accepted into the bourgeois traditional art elite at the Academy of Arts. Hitler always felt superior to people from a working-class background, and he was 'determined' not to slip down the social scale – as he saw it – and become associated with that class. As a result, he was determined to avoid taking any job associated with the working classes in general and anything that involved hard manual work in particular. One person who met Hitler during his Vienna period later told of how he would often show a picture of his late father, wearing the grand uniform of the Imperial Customs Service, in order to emphasise – in a rather insecure manner – his middle-class background and its supposed 'respectability'.

Hitler had no desire to look for a mundane job, and he did not want to return to Linz as a failure. So he stayed in Vienna, unsure of what to do with the rest of his life. He made no effort to gain a full-time job, nor did he come forward to undertake his compulsory military service in the Austrian armed forces – as he was legally obliged to do – in the summer of 1909. From the autumn of 1908 until the late summer months of 1909, he lived in three different flats. In the mild autumn of 1909, he briefly lived rough, mostly sleeping on park benches. Exactly why he needed to live in this way remains unclear. One possibility is that the savings from his inheritance finally ran out. A more convincing explanation as to why Hitler slept rough in the autumn of 1909 is that he knew he was now eligible for conscription into the Austrian army. In sum, Hitler's brief period as a 'down and out' in Vienna, which lasted less than three months, was really a means of avoiding being conscripted into the army.

In October 1909, Hitler took up residence in the Meidling, a men's hostel funded by a wealthy Jewish family. We also know he undertook a few odd jobs at this time: he cleared some snow, carried luggage for passengers at a local railway station, and worked for a couple of days as a building labourer. At the hostel he was befriended by Reinhold Hanisch, an unemployed ex-domestic servant and 'artist', perhaps of the bar-room variety. Hanisch described Hitler when he first caught sight of him as shabbily dressed and incapable of organising his own life. Hanisch persuaded him to write a letter to one of his relatives for some money to buy artists' materials, and then set himself up as a commercial artist. Hanisch promised to sell Hitler's paintings and postcards in return for a commission on each sale. Hitler did write to his ever-loyal Aunt Johanna, who sent him 50 Kronen by return of post. With this money, Hitler bought an overcoat and some artists' materials.

In December 1909, Hitler – accompanied by Hanisch – moved to the Mannerheim, a much smarter lodging house occupied by working men on limited incomes. The residents of this 'Home for Men' paid nearly 3 Kronen a week for a small room (which had to be vacated during working hours). In return, they gained access to the many other facilities on offer, which included a large dining room, a reading room, a shower room and a laundry. As Hitler was not allowed to paint in his own room, he did so on a small table by a window in the lounge area. This was, of course, a great come-down for someone who had aspired to become a 'great artist'. Yet Hitler's time at the Mannerheim actually strengthened his personality and infused him with a belief that life was a constant struggle in which only those with great willpower and strength of character could hope to survive.

Those who knew Hitler at the Mannerheim in the years from 1909 to 1913 later described him as a 'loner', and someone who held extremely dog-matic opinions on almost every subject imaginable. During the time he spent at the hostel, he completed between 700 and 800 paintings, drawings and postcards, most of which were copied from other people's work and sold in nearby shops, taverns, cafés and art shops. In addition, he produced several advertising posters for local businesses, including one for an anti-perspirant foot powder called 'Teddy's'.

By the end of 1910, it is estimated that Hitler was earning 70–80 Kronen a month from the sales of his artwork. There are also strong indications that his income was further boosted by a substantial gift of 3800 Kronen from his aunt Johanna. A further sign of his healthy financial state was his decision to transfer his orphan's pension (which he had fraudulently continued to receive by claiming he was a 'student' at the Vienna School of Art) of 24 Kronen per month to his half-sister, Angela.

However, the partnership between Hitler and the streetwise Hanisch lasted only eight months. It ended because Hitler thought his painting of the Vienna parliament building had been sold for 50 crowns, not the 10 crowns which Hanisch claimed he had received for it. Hitler felt he had been cheated and he took legal proceedings against Hanisch. During the hearing of the case – which took place on 11 August 1910 – Hitler claimed Hanisch was 'a practised liar' who was registered at the Mannerheim under the false name of Fritz Walter. At the end of the court proceedings, Hanisch was sentenced to seven days in jail. In the 1930s, Hanisch sold the story of his brief and tempestuous relationship with Hitler to the popular press. In 1936, Hanisch was arrested by the Gestapo and charged with spreading 'libellous stories about Hitler'. On 4 February 1937, he was found dead in his cell, reportedly from a heart attack, but there are strong indications he was murdered by the Gestapo (probably on Hitler's orders).

HITLER'S POLITICAL IDEAS IN VIENNA

In *Mein Kampf*, Hitler claimed he was keenly interested in political developments in Vienna. But he belonged to no political party and kept up to date on political matters by reading newspapers, periodicals and cheap pamphlets. His major interests were in the less openly political areas of music, art and architecture. It seems Hitler's political views in this period were pretty similar to those of upper-class elites and lower-middle-class groups who felt threatened by the growth of socialist ideas. Before Hitler came to Vienna, he was certainly a fervent nationalist, who identified with the Protestant German Reich rather than the multinational Hapsburg Empire, even though he was himself a Catholic.

Hitler later claimed two political figures had a profound influence upon his political 'awakening' in Vienna: Georg von Schöenerer, leader of the Pan-German Nationalist Party, and Karl Lueger, the leader of the Christian Social Party. Schöenerer's Pan-German Party, unlike its German equivalent, was not preoccupied with German imperial expansion outside Europe, but instead championed the idea of all Germans living in a single state. Schöenerer was deeply anti-Semitic, regarding 'the Jews' as responsible for all the evils of the world, and demanding special 'anti-Jewish laws' to prevent the further growth of Jewish influence in Austrian society. The major weaknesses of Schöenerer as a politician, according to Hitler, were his inability to arouse – or even seek – the support of the masses and his complete failure to gain support for his political ideas from the powerful institutions of the state: the army, the church and the bureaucracy.

It was Dr Karl Lueger, the popular leader of the Christian Social Party and mayor of Vienna, who made an even greater impression on the young Hitler. It was not the political programme of this Austrian demagogue that attracted Hitler. In fact, he thought Lueger had too much faith in the multinational Austrian state, and did not champion German nationalist ideas passionately enough. What Hitler admired most about Lueger were his oratorical abilities and his pragmatic approach to political problems. Lueger was a populist leader, who pursued his political objectives in a pragmatic and flexible manner. He was willing to exploit his political ideologies – some of which he did not believe in – in order to win over voters. The group he aimed his oratory towards as Mayor of Vienna were the backbone of the lower middle class: white-collar workers, Catholic workers, artisans, local government officials and shopkeepers, but his oratory also proved attractive to sections of the upper middle class, who were usually attracted to conservative parties. Above all, Hitler was impressed by Lueger's ability to appeal to the ordinary voter through powerful slogans such as 'We must do something for the Little Man!'

Hitler was already a fervent anti-Marxist during his time in Vienna. He had a 'great hatred' of the Social Democratic Party, because of the devotion of its supporters to socialist ideas. Yet there were aspects of the socialist left he did admire, particularly the ability of the Social Democratic Party to make effective use of propaganda to attract the masses and its ability to go out on the streets in demonstrations and parades, carrying flags and banners to emphasise the strength and unity of its supporters. Hitler believed that only by challenging the socialists 'on the streets' could they be stopped from winning over the masses to their ideas.

Hitler claimed in *Mein Kampf* that the idea of combining the extreme German nationalism of Schöenerer with the charismatic leadership of Leuger and the popular street fighting and propaganda abilities of the socialists to form a 'National Socialist' Party was already forming in his mind during his period in Vienna. It is clear such a party was primarily viewed – by Hitler – as a popular alternative to the rise of socialist ideas. Yet we only have Hitler's word for it that his political ideas were so clear at this time in his life. It is probably more accurate to suggest these views about his political ideas in Vienna were self-serving rhetoric, designed to portray himself as a man of crystal clear vision, when in reality he had no independently thought out political ideas of his own. In reality, Hitler was an interested political spectator in Vienna who had not even contemplated a career in politics.

HITLER'S ANTI-SEMITISM IN VIENNA

It is also important to assess Hitler's attitude towards 'the Jews' during his Vienna period, given the importance of his ideas on this subject to the later history of the Nazi Party. Surprisingly, there is little evidence in Hitler's early life to suggest that an ingrained prejudice against Jews was a dominant preoccupation. On the contrary, the sincere feelings Hitler expressed towards

Dr Bloch, a Jewish doctor, for the care he offered his mother during her terminal illness do not indicate a congenital hatred of all Jewish people. Hitler admits to being tolerant of Jews while he lived in Linz, often expressing 'repugnance' whenever he heard strong expressions of anti-Semitism. On the other hand, Kubizek, his close friend, does recall Hitler being somewhat prejudiced towards Jews in Linz and Vienna, but he does not think he was an extreme anti-Semite during the time he knew him [*Doc. 1*].

It was during his Vienna period that Hitler's feelings about Jews started to change. According to Hitler himself, he went from being a 'weak-kneed cosmopolitan' to a 'fanatical anti-Semite' during this time (Fest, 1974: 39). What prompted Hitler's growing hatred towards the Jews is a subject of deep historical significance. Hitler claimed his rising resentment towards Jews was – at first – prompted by seeing Jews 'everywhere' on the streets of Vienna and concluding they bore 'no resemblance to Germans' [*Doc. 1*]. This visual dislike of the Jew as an 'alien' force in Vienna was strongly reinforced by Hitler's subsequent reading of many popular anti-Semitic pamphlets and newspapers. He appears to have swallowed whole the prevailing views of this cheap anti-Semitic literature, which blamed the Jews for every sin and vice in multicultural Vienna. One key aspect of the gutter anti-Semitic press in Vienna was its continual stress on Jews being heavily involved in running the vice trade in the city. Anti-Semitic pamphlets were full of stories of 'racially unfit' Jews seducing 'innocent German maidens'.

It has been suggested that one of the roots of Hitler's virulent anti-Semitism may have been a tortured sexual envy, prompted by seeing Jewish men, even of advancing years, seducing young girls, whom Hitler did not even have the courage to talk to. Hitler's sexual relations in Vienna are a mystery. One person who met Hitler during his Vienna period – and whose evidence is considered very unreliable – suggested Hitler had sex with prostitutes in Vienna, and was obsessed with defecation and urination as part of the sex act. Yet another witness from the Vienna period, equally unreliable, claims Hitler attempted – unsuccessfully – to rape a young model while she was posing in a life-drawing class. More recently, Lothar Machtan, a German historian, has controversially argued that Hitler was a (repressed) homosexual, who had sex with 'rent boys' during his Vienna period (Machtan, 2001). It is, however, far more likely that Hitler had no sexual contact with either men or women during his entire time in Vienna.

Another possibility, and a more plausible one, is that a virulent, all-consuming anti-Semitism did not dominate Hitler's political – or sexual – thinking during his Vienna period. Hitler was certainly attracted to anti-Semitic ideas at this time, but this was true of the majority of supporters of German nationalism. It is more doubtful that Hitler's anti-Semitism was an all-consuming 'master idea' at that juncture in his life. For a so-called 'passionate' anti-Semite, some of Hitler's behaviour in Vienna was extremely odd. He regularly attended musical evenings at the home of a Jewish family. Most of his closest acquaintances at the Mannerheim, including those he most trusted, were Jewish. It is also known he preferred to sell his paintings through Jewish art dealers, because he regarded them as the most honest to deal with.

MUNICH, 1913–14

In May 1913, Adolf Hitler, then aged 24, suddenly ended his lonely and very unsuccessful period in Vienna. He travelled by train across the Austrian border to the German city of Munich. Hitler's fateful relationship with Germany and its people had now begun. Yet a patriotic love of Germany was not the major reason for his departure from the Austrian capital. Hitler – who had successfully avoided conscription for over four years – feared he was about to be called up for military service. He registered with the Munich police as 'stateless' rather than as an 'Austrian citizen', as he was legally required to do. The documents relating to Hitler's failure to enlist in the army show the Austrian military authorities had been searching in vain for him for some considerable time. At no time between 1909 and 1913 had Hitler ever presented himself to undertake his military service. Police files relating to the case reveal that he had not registered his address in Vienna with the police in Linz. The police eventually discovered he had gone to live in Vienna from interviews with people in Linz who knew him. They soon made inquiries at the Mannerheim – and found he had already left there for Munich. In January 1914, the Austrian police finally tracked him down – with the assistance of the German criminal police – to a Munich address (34 Schleissheimer Strasse) in a poor area of the city, where he had taken lodgings with the family of Joseph Popp, a tailor, at a cost of 20 marks a month. The charge of 'draft dodging' (most famously associated later with American peace-loving 'hippies' in the 1960s) was a very serious one in Austria in 1914 and carried a lengthy prison sentence. Hitler was asked to go to Salzburg (on 5 February 1914) to explain why he had avoided service for so long. In a written statement presented to the recruitment board, he claimed he had not come forward for military service in the autumn of 1909 because he was 'a very inexperienced man, without any financial aid' and 'no other companion but eternally gnawing hunger'. He also claimed he had submitted his documents for military service, but they must have been lost in the post. Of course, these explanations were extremely weak. There is little doubt he deliberately – and consciously – avoided military service. Yet the Salzburg recruitment panel accepted his explanation. In the end, they decided Hitler was 'unfit' and 'too weak' for military service because of a minor lung complaint. He later claimed he was a 'draft dodger' not because he was a coward – more likely, he was just plain lazy – but because he did not want to join the Austrian army, as he felt great animosity towards the Austro-Hungarian empire and a greater affinity for Germany.

Hitler describes the brief time he spent in Munich before the First World War as 'the happiest and by far the most contented of my life' (Bullock, 1962: 48). Munich enjoyed the reputation before 1914 of being a charming, artistic, light-hearted and culturally open city. Hitler's life in Munich followed much the same shapeless pattern as it had done in Vienna. He remained without close friends and made no contacts with the art world or local political groups. He liked Munich because it was a 'German city', very different from ethnically diverse Vienna.

The members of the Popp family, with whom Hitler lived, later recalled Hitler as leading a solitary existence. He mostly painted postcards and watercolours, which he sold to local dealers. He also borrowed many books from the local library. Hitler was able to command an income of 120 marks per month – a modest income, but one which allowed him to live tolerably. During the day he would also sit reading newspapers in local cafés, mostly drinking coffee, and occasionally indulging his lifelong love of chocolate cake. By this time, Hitler appears to have realised he was not going to be a great artist. He painted to earn a modest living, and planned to pursue academic studies in order to become an architect.

THE FIRST WORLD WAR

The event which truly transformed Hitler's life was the outbreak of the First World War. 'I am not ashamed to say', Hitler later wrote in *Mein Kampf*, 'carried away by the enthusiasm of the moment, I sank down on my knees and thanked heaven out of the fullness of my heart for granting me the good fortune of being permitted to live in such a time' (Toland, 1976: 46). Many historians view Hitler as a logical consequence of deep-seated flaws in German historical development. Yet Hitler's rise to power was more a consequence of the German defeat in the First World War than anything else. Without the war, and the fact that Germany lost it, it is almost certain Hitler would never have entered politics and the Nazi Party would never have needed to exist.

Hitler volunteered on 3 August 1914 to serve in the German army. He was accepted by the 16th Bavarian Infantry Regiment (known as the 'List' Regiment) in spite of his Austrian citizenship, and he spent most of the war on the Western front as a dispatch runner, carrying messages between the officer staff at HQ and front-line troops. Hitler was not a soldier in the trenches, but his job, a solitary one – which suited his personality – was hazardous. Many dispatch riders (usually riding bicycles, but sometimes motorcycles in the latter stages of the war) were killed by enemy fire while trying to deliver their vital messages.

Hitler's passionate involvement with the fate of the German army during the First World War was the real turning point in his life. Hitler described this as 'the most memorable period of my life' (Bullock, 1962: 50). The war not only gave Hitler a means of showing his nationalist passion for the German cause, but also offered him the opportunity to escape from boredom, frustration and failure. It gave his life a new purpose and energy: he was now a soldier fighting for the country he loved.

The army was for Hitler a surrogate home and family. During the war, Hitler claimed he had no worries. He took orders from officers without a word of comment, nor did he ever question the decisions taken by his officers or the aims of the war. Whenever he heard of acts of humanity displayed by German soldiers towards the enemy (such as the famous 1914 Christmas Day football match in no man's land between British and German soldiers) he expressed outrage. He was respected by his officers as 'loyal and obedient'.

Hitler's fellow soldiers in the List Regiment thought 'Adi' (their nickname for him) 'eccentric'. They noticed he could often sit for hours, silently brooding or reading, but would occasionally jump to his feet and break into a 'wild monologue', usually bemoaning anyone who showed a lack of patriotism towards the German war effort. He never complained about the mud, the filth and the lack of food on the front line. One certain way of hearing Hitler's loudest angry rhetoric was to suggest Germany might actually lose the war. Many fellow soldiers, though not completely disliking him, often found his unquestioning patriotism irritating. As one put it: 'We cursed him and found him intolerable' (Shirer, 1961: 48). Hitler never asked for leave, did not receive letters from home (not even at Christmas), and never gave any details of his early life to his comrades in arms. He would often shake his head when hearing light-hearted remarks or jokes. He was not at all interested, when on leave, in seeking the company of women or engaging in the sexual banter which was then commonplace among his fellow soldiers. His closest companion during the war was a stray dog he adopted called Foxl. On political matters, his fellow soldiers claimed he had very little to say. No one can remember him mentioning his so-called 'ingrained anti-Semitism'. Photographs taken of Hitler during the war show him with a dour, fixed expression on his face. He appears isolated from the other soldiers, and looks much older than in his mid-20s.

Yet it must be admitted that Hitler was a very good soldier. His coolness under fire earned him a reputation of 'invulnerability' among his fellow soldiers. In August 1914, he was awarded the Iron Cross (2nd class). In August 1918, he received the Iron Cross (1st Class). The latter award, given on the recommendation of a Jewish officer, was a very prestigious one, and was rarely given to a volunteer soldier. Accounts vary as to why Hitler received it. One account claims he took fifteen British soldiers prisoner. But the official history of the List Regiment gives no details about the specific act of bravery for which it was awarded. The award of the Iron Cross was very important for Hitler's later political career as a German nationalist. It gave tangible evidence of his bravery. Given his obvious devotion to duty, it is surprising he was never promoted above the rank of lance-corporal. A senior officer of the List Regiment, when giving evidence at the Nuremberg war trials, said the question of promoting Hitler had often cropped up, but it was rejected because 'we could discover no leadership qualities in him' (Fest, 1974: 69).

In October 1916, Hitler was wounded in the left thigh during the Battle of the Somme. He was sent to Beelitz hospital in Berlin to recover from his injury. In Berlin, after his discharge from the hospital, he noticed people 'boasting of their own cowardice' and a general atmosphere of discontent and defeatism. On a visit to Munich shortly afterwards he 'could no longer recognise the city' and noticed 'every clerk was a Jew' (Hitler, 1936: 87). He became increasingly filled with fury against politicians, journalists, Jews and left-wing radicals who were constantly talking of defeat. Hitler returned to the front, convinced the German war effort was being severely undermined by 'Jews and Marxists' at home.

Hitler took part in the final offensive of the German army in 1918. On the evening of 18 October 1918 south of Ypres, he was briefly blinded in a mustard gas attack, and was transported to Pasewalk hospital in Pomerania to recover. In November 1918, a pastor told patients that a revolution had broken out in Germany, the Kaiser had abdicated, a republic had been declared, and the war had been lost. On hearing this news, Hitler – for the first time since he stood over his mother's grave – began to cry. 'It became impossible for me to sit still one minute more', Hitler later recalled, 'and everything went black again before my eyes. I tottered and groped my way back to the dormitory, threw myself on my bunk, and dug my burning head into my blanket and pillow ... So it had all been in vain' (Fest, 1974: 78).

Hitler later claimed this was the exact moment when he decided to enter politics, in order to rid Germany of the 'wretched gang of Socialists, Jews, and democratic politicians' who had 'stabbed Germany in the back' and robbed it of victory. The end of the war was also a very personal blow to Hitler. It meant he had no work, no home, no friends, and no job. In reality, Hitler – fully aware of the powerlessness of his position – did not really make up his mind to enter politics as soon as he heard of Germany's defeat. All he decided to do, since he had nowhere else to go, nor any real idea of what the future held, was to stay in the army, even though the army in Bavaria at the time was run by the 'Soldiers' Councils' he supposedly despised. When he did take his first active steps into politics, over a year after the war ended, it was on the orders of an army officer. As with most of the acts of Hitler's early life, the reality was very different from the myth.

CHAPTER THREE

THE EARLY GROWTH OF THE NAZI PARTY

On 21 November 1918, Hitler returned to Munich in a dispirited state of mind to contemplate an uncertain future. When he arrived, he found the city in a state of political crisis. The Bavarian monarchy, which had been a feature of Bavarian political life for a thousand years, had already been toppled. The Bavarian People's Republic, composed of a group of socialist revolutionaries led by Kurt Eisner, a diminutive, bearded, Jewish Social Democrat, promised 'government by kindness'. A sizeable number of the leading personalities in the new government were Jewish intellectuals who were strongly attached to Marxist ideals. It might be expected that Hitler, given his supposed bitter anti-Marxist and anti-Semitic views, would have nothing to do with this type of socialist rule, and engage in counter-revolutionary activities. Yet he did nothing of the sort. In fact, Hitler tolerated the new socialist – and Jewish-dominated – Bavarian government for a personal, selfish and opportunistic reason: he wanted to stay in the army. It did not seem to matter to him that the Munich regiment in which he served was under the control of a left-wing 'Soldiers' Council'. It was not the first, nor would it be the last, occasion when Hitler would compromise his so-called 'unshakable principles' in order to do what he wanted.

The 'socialist experiment' in Munich, built on the extraordinary revolutionary mood which swept through Germany at the end of the First World War, soon collapsed. The new government favoured democratic rule, but did not purge nationalist and anti-democratic groups within the army, the civil service, the police force and the judiciary. As a result, the forces of the Bavarian right regrouped. On 21 February 1919, Eisner, while walking to the Bavarian parliament, was gunned down by a young right-wing Munich University student with aristocratic connections, Graf Anton von Arco-Valley. This provocative political assassination prompted communist leaders to call a general strike. In April, the socialists established a communist-style 'Soviet Council' led by Rudolf Eglhofer and his 'Red Army'. The level of violence between left and right in Bavaria intensified. On 29 April 1920, eight prisoners of the Red Army, including some members of the right-wing Thule Society, were brutally murdered. This crime galvanised most of the right-wing elements in Bavarian society into an explosive counter-reaction. The result was a four-day mini 'civil war' during which troops from the army, supported by the Free Corps (Freikorps) consisting of hundreds of patriotic, wild-eyed, trigger-happy ex-soldiers armed with hand grenades and rifles – supplied from army stocks – quickly suppressed the short-lived workers' revolt in a bloody struggle that left most of the communist leaders (among them Elghofer) wounded or dead. The final death toll in this brief but bloody Bavarian conflict was 606, including 335 civilians. Most of these were communists and socialists. A 'moderate' Social Democratic (SPD) government was put back in power. But this was swiftly replaced by an extreme right-wing nationalist govern-ment led by Gustav von Kahr, supported by the reactionary local leaders of the German army.

THE BIRTH OF THE NAZI PARTY

After the demise of the 'red dictatorship', everything changed in Bavarian politics. The region became a right-wing Noah's Ark in which every type of snarling nationalist found refuge. Hitler, although he took no active part in crushing the left in Bavaria, was now in the perfect place to make his mark on the political stage. It must be understood, however, that his first move into politics was not even his own idea. In May 1919, he was selected by Captain Karl Mayr to become an Instruction Officer in the Information Department of the district command of the army. Mayr later described Hitler as 'a stray dog looking for a master ... ready to throw in his lot with anyone who would show him kindness' (Kershaw, 1998: 122). The Information Department had been given government funding to create a group of reliable pro-nationalist agents whose main task was to indoctrin-ate officers and soldiers with nationalist and anti-communist ideas. In June 1919, Hitler was sent by his army superiors on a week-long course on 'anti-Bolshevism' at Munich University. During the course, Hitler heard a number of pro-nationalist lectures, including one that greatly impressed him: 'Breaking Interest Slavery', delivered by Gottfried Feder, a Pan-German economics lecturer who told the students that 'productive capital' in large German-run industries should be encouraged, but 'rapacious capital', which he associated with 'Jews', should be 'eliminated' from the German economy. It seems Hitler made a favourable impression on Feder on the course, as he told Mayr shortly afterwards about Hitler's 'natural' speaking abilities, displayed during the discussion sessions which followed each lecture. In August 1919, Hitler, given the role of Educational Officer by Mayr, was asked to 'instruct' troops on a five-day course at a local army camp on the dangers of communism. On this course, Hitler discovered his greatest talent: he was an excellent, dramatic and passionate speaker, with a popular manner which immediately struck a chord with his listeners. It was the realisation of his natural ability as a public speaker that first propelled Hitler towards the idea of becoming actively engaged in politics.

In September 1918, Mayr gave Hitler the task of spying on the many small right- and left-wing political parties and radical debating societies operating in the Munich area during this fraught period. Hitler was 'ordered' by Mayr to go and observe a gathering of the German Workers' Party (the Deutsche Arbeiterpartei, or DAP) held in a Munich beer hall (the Sterneckbrau). The DAP had been set up by Anton Drexler, a locksmith who worked for a rail company, and Karl Harrer, a local right-wing journalist. The party first appeared at the end of the First World War as the Workers' Political Society, a small discussion group with a restricted membership of just seven people. Drexler wanted the group to become a political party which appealed to the public. On 5 January 1919, therefore, the DAP became a political party. It started to organise meetings, and was always on the lookout for new members.

The small inner core of activists in the DAP mostly met in the small, dimly lit back rooms of beer halls. The DAP struck a strongly nationalist, anti-Semitic and anti-capitalist tone. It had a democratic constitution: the membership elected the executive committee, discussions took place on policy issues, and votes decided the party line adopted. Yet the DAP, led by Drexler, lacking in funds and members, stood little chance of becoming a major political party. The first time Hitler attended a meeting of the DAP, on Friday 12 September 1919, the keynote speaker was Gottfried Feder, who gave the lecture on 'interest slavery' that Hitler had already heard at Munich University. In the brief discussion which followed, Professor Baumann, the second invited speaker, suggested it would be a good idea for Bavaria to break away from Germany. This prompted Hitler to launch a strong verbal attack on Baumann's views. Drexler was so impressed by Hitler's interjection in the debate that he made a point of going up to him at the end of the meeting, invited him to join the party, took his name and address, then pressed a copy of his self-penned pamphlet *My Political Awakening* into his hand [*Doc. 2*]. Once more, it was Hitler's brilliant speaking ability that had caught the eye and attracted the listener.

Hitler was not impressed by what he saw at the poorly attended meeting of the DAP. It was little different in its political stance from many similar *Volkisch* nationalist groups operating in Munich at the time. Hitler was more attracted by Drexler's pamphlet, which he read, unable to sleep, just before dawn on the following morning. It told the story of how this humble locksmith had created a new political party, combining nationalism with some anti-capitalist and 'socialist' ideas. Yet the major aim of the party was to weaken the appeal of Marxism and socialism among the working classes, Hitler claimed he was already thinking of creating a political party along similar lines even before he went to observe the meeting of the DAP. Hence, when a postcard arrived a few days after the meeting he had attended inviting him to join the committee of the DAP, he accepted. Hitler later claimed he decided to join because he thought this small, ill-organised and little known party could be moulded to suit his own purposes. According to the Hitler myth, he was the seventh member of the party, but when his membership card was later found in the German archives, it was discovered his membership number was 515.

Hitler's own account of his motivation for joining the DAP must also be treated with great caution. His claim to have wrestled with nagging doubts about joining the party hardly seems credible when all the facts are considered. Mayr, his army boss, whose account is far more reliable, says he 'ordered' Hitler to join, so the party could be used as a propaganda vehicle for the army, to bolster its drive to weaken the appeal of socialism among the workers. It also seems clear that army funds, probably channelled through Hitler after he joined the party, were used to enable Hitler to book local halls as speaking venues for the party, and to finance expensive newspaper advertisements. In fact, during Hitler's early active period as a member of the DAP, from September 1919 to April 1920, he continued to draw his army salary, and he stopped his surveillance activities on other right- and left-wing parties. This suggests the army had decided to 'plant' Hitler in the DAP to build up its popularity. It seems reasonable to conclude, therefore, that it was Mayr and his fellow officers who decided the DAP's novel combination of nationalism and socialism could be used as a suitable army vehicle – under Hitler's leadership – for its own anti-socialist propaganda. No doubt other 'political instructors' made their way into the Nazi Party – and other right-wing parties – under similar orders. We know, for example, that Hermann Esser, Mayr's press agent, became an important speaker and propagandist in the early Nazi Party. Hitler's move into politics was really the result of an order from the army, not part of a fully thought out plan of his own. Accordingly, he began his career in politics as a willing tool of anti-democratic forces within the Munich command of the army.

Hitler now had a field of action for his passionate love of Germany, his propaganda skill, and, especially, his brilliant speaking ability. His entry into politics gave him a new lease of life. He immediately – and energetically – threw himself into his role as the chief propagandist of the infant party. Within a matter of weeks, Hitler transformed the DAP from a German lounge bar ranting club into a noisy local nationalist party, fond of creating a public outcry. On 16 October 1919, Hitler organised a public meeting of the DAP which was attended by 111 people.

Hitler's speeches at subsequent public meetings helped to increase the profile and membership of the DAP which was not what Hitler said – most right-wing hotheads said much the same – but the way he said it – in a manner reminiscent of fundamentalist religious fanatics, evoking melancholy images of suffering and despair, willing to give his life for a cause – that set him apart as a public speaker, put the Nazi Party on the map of local Munich politics, and salvaged Hitler from a career that seemed to be heading for the scrapyard of under-achievers.

In his speeches, Hitler cast himself in the role of an alienated, bitter and resentful 'outsider' from the 'new Germany'. He had the ability to inspire an audience to share his bitterness, his fears, his self-pity and his frustrations, and he also inspired them to support his 'positive' programme to rescue Germany from the 'cowards and traitors' who had 'betrayed the Fatherland' [*Doc. 9*]. In doing so, Hitler gave his listeners a dream that 'tomorrow belonged to them'. He built up this longing for a better tomorrow on the foundation of deep feelings of unhappiness and bitterness over the German defeat in the war. He blamed that defeat on those people at home who he claimed had 'stabbed Germany in the back'. Every ex-soldier still depressed about Germany's defeat and in sympathy with nationalist ideas could easily identify with Hitler's outbursts of loathing against the 'November criminals', the 'profiteering Jews' and the Treaty of Versailles [*Doc. 4*]. All of Hitler's speeches built towards a feverish, hysterical climax, usually ending with the phrase 'There is only defiance and hate, hate and again hate'.

Hitler soon became indispensable to this small right-wing fringe party. He was not only the most effective public speaker in the party but its most effective organiser and propagandist. He put the party on a more business-like footing by renting an office above the Sterneckbräu and installing in it a telephone, a safe, a filing cabinet and a typewriter. A rubber stamp bearing the party name and printed membership cards were also purchased. Hitler put a great deal of effort into improving the advertising of the party. He was involved in designing striking red posters and leaflets for the party which were posted around Munich.

It was also Hitler who insisted the party should take its message to larger audiences, something older members of the party committee were not very enthusiastic about doing. The large gatherings of the party were never peaceful. On the contrary, they provoked confrontation with left-wing opponents, generated passion from supporters, and injected the much-needed oxygen of publicity into the party. A substantial number of young people were attracted to meetings of the party by the action, excitement, and many opportunities for violence they offered.

On 24 February 1920, one of the first large meetings of the party which Hitler had publicised through advertising in the local press attracted an audience of 2000 people. At the meeting, which was held at the Hofbräuhaus, Hitler outlined the 25-point party programme drafted by

Feder, Drexler and Hitler himself [*Doc. 3*]. Not long after this meeting, the DAP changed its name to the National Socialist German Workers' Party (the Nationalsozialistische Deutsche Arbeiterpartei, or NSDAP), which became commonly known as the Nazi Party, adopting as its party symbol, at Hitler's insistence, the now infamous swastika. On 1 April 1920, Hitler finally left the army, with the intention of seizing the leadership of the Nazi Party and making it the instrument of his own particular brand of extreme nationalism.

THE EARLY PROGRAMME OF THE NAZI PARTY

The 25 points of the Nazi Party were declared 'unalterable', but they were mostly ignored when Hitler came to power. The party's most notable gimmick was to combine right-wing, nationalist and anti-Semitic ideas with some anti-capitalist, so-called 'socialist' measures. This novel combination allowed the Nazi Party a banner under which workers could shelter alongside middle- and upper-class groups, thereby providing an effective bulwark against communist revolution at home and offering the possibility of restoring German military power in the world.

The 'nationalist' elements of the party programme included promises to revise the 'hated' Treaty of Versailles, unite all German speakers into an expanded Greater German Reich, exclude Jews from 'German' citizenship rights, take control of the press, and build a 'strong' nationalist government under the direction of an all-powerful leader. The 'socialist' parts of the platform included pledges to nationalise trusts, abolish land rents, restrict interest on loans, introduce profit sharing in industry, open up large department stores to small traders, confiscate profits made by industry during war, and create a People's Army [*Doc. 3*]. The 'anti-capitalist' elements in the programme appeared to spell the end of interest-bearing loans. One striking omission was the complete neglect – apart from a brief mention of land reform – of the plight of agriculture. The broad principles of the party programme were never substantially challenged or altered during the period of the Nazi rise to power.

The 'nationalist' parts of the programme were not dissimilar to those championed by other nationalist groups. But they were – for the most part – supported by Hitler, who implemented many of them after he came to power. What really distinguished the Nazi Party platform from other right-wing fringe groups – and gave it a distinctive appeal – was its advocacy of certain so-called 'socialist' and 'anti-capitalist' policies. These proposed 'socialist' measures were supported by many members of the party. But Hitler viewed most of them as mere window dressing, designed to attract 'dumb' workers to the party. This view is reinforced by the knowledge that hardly any of the 'socialist' elements of the Nazi Party programme were implemented after 1933. Hitler was quite prepared – as his time in the Information Department of the army had taught him – to use the slogans and symbols of socialism to gain support for extreme nationalism.

THE EMERGENCE OF HITLER AS LEADER OF THE NAZI PARTY

By the end of 1920, Nazi Party membership had grown to 3000, largely as a result of Hitler's public speeches and his energetic propaganda efforts. In December 1920, the Nazi Party bought a local newspaper (the *Münchener Beobachter*) for 180,000 marks, renaming it the *Völkischer Beobachter* (*Racial Observer*) soon afterwards. The large sum of money used to buy the official party newspaper came from Dietrich Eckart, a poet and publicist, some prominent Munich conservatives, and a 60,000-mark donation from secret army funds. It was the purchase of the *Völkischer Beobachter* that greatly increased Hitler's dominance over the party, as he used the paper as the chief agency of party propaganda, and as a means of transmitting orders and directives to local party activists.

By this time, Hitler had surrounded himself with a team of people who became the nucleus of the Nazi Party leadership, most notably: Alfred Rosenberg, the self-styled party philosopher, who championed the racial theories of the party, especially its pronounced anti-Semitic views; Max Amann, Hitler's former army sergeant, who became the publishing manager; Eckart, who had a severe alcohol problem but who provided Hitler with much-needed funding and contacts; and Captain Ernst Roehm (introduced to Hitler by Mayr), a tough and menacing bully boy who recruited thousands of ex-soldiers and members of the paramilitary Freikorps to form the Nazi storm troopers (the Sturmabteilungen, or SA), a private army which grew into a fearsome street fighting force. Roehm replaced Mayr as Hitler's chief link with the local army command, and provided useful contacts for the Nazi Party within the army and among like-minded 'patriotic associations'. Hermann Goering, a highly decorated fighter pilot, was also useful in introducing Hitler to many important figures in Bavarian high society. Another important early recruit to the Nazi cause was Rudolf Hess, who had been awarded the Iron Cross 1st Class, and became Hitler's personal secretary. Indeed, so many ex-soldiers were involved in the Nazi Party, or more likely were encouraged to become involved by their army superiors, it was more like an army propaganda unit supported by a paramilitary private army than a conventional political party.

With a band of loyal supporters around him, Hitler pressed for the 'committee based' structure, supported by the 'old guard' in the party, to be replaced by a command structure in which a single leader would have complete control over party decision making. Under this proposal, any party member wanting to challenge the leader's views, or alter the party programme, faced immediate expulsion [*Doc. 5*]. At the first national congress of the Nazi Party, held in Munich on 21 January 1921, Drexler claimed Hitler's desire for strong leadership was really a disguised bid for the leadership of the party, and the proposal to change the structure of the party was rejected.

In the spring of 1921, in a move designed to weaken Hitler's stranglehold over the party, Drexler held secret talks with the German Socialist Party (the Deutsch-Sozialistische Partei, or DDP) founded by Alfred Brunner, an engineer from Düsseldorf, concerning a possible merger of the two nationalist parties. These negotiations went as far as agreeing the headquarters of the merged party, which would be in Berlin – not Munich. Not surprisingly, Hitler was strongly opposed to the merger plans, which, if implemented, would have threatened his supremacy over the tightly knit Munich-based Nazi Party. Instead of attempting to win the argument through discussion, Hitler took the prima donna option and threw a temper tantrum. On 11 July 1920, totally unwilling to compromise, he resigned from the Nazi Party. The initial response of the party committee to Hitler's resignation was to publish a pamphlet accusing Hitler of wanting to become a 'party dictator', criticising his 'bohemian' way of life, and even suggesting (unbelievably) that Hitler was in 'the pay of the Jews'. In response, Hitler set out his own uncompromising personal terms for rejoining the party: he wanted to be elected 'party chairman' with 'dictatorial powers'. Drexler and the other members of the committee, soon realising the loss of their star speaker was a potentially mortal blow to the party, and fearing he might establish a popular rival party of his own, decided to accede to Hitler's demands. At a specially convened national congress of the Nazi Party which opened on 29 July 1921, the proposal that Hitler be given 'dictatorial' control over the party was carried by 553 votes to 1.

THE GROWTH OF THE 'FÜHRER CULT'

In a very short space of time, Hitler had taken complete control of the Nazi Party. He quickly attempted to bring local branches of the party outside the Munich area under his control by issuing 'directives' to them. At first, local party activists, accustomed to having discussions on issues and passing resolutions, disregarded Hitler's orders. But they soon relented. In January 1922, for example, Hitler won a massive vote of confidence from the party membership for a proposal that all branches of the party should be subordinate to the personal will of the leader and directives from the central party headquarters in Munich. As Hitler's power over the party increased, all semblance of autonomy previously enjoyed by local branches disappeared. At the end of 1922, Hitler created the post of delegate in charge of a local branch of the party, who was expected to ensure the decisions of the leader were enacted at the local level.

Under Hitler's leadership, from 1921 to 1923 the Nazi Party became the most vocal supporter of the idea of overthrowing the democratic Weimar Republic by force. To further this aim, Hitler enhanced the status and role of the SA under the leadership of Ernst Roehm. Previously, the SA had been little more than a rowdy mob of bouncers whose main role was to keep order at Nazi Party meetings. After Hitler took complete charge of the Nazi Party, the SA was turned into a loud and raging paramilitary force, ready and willing to 'rescue Germany'. Under Roehm's shrewd leadership, the SA improved its relations with the other paramilitary groups operating in the Munich region. Hence, the Nazi Party under Hitler operated not the politics of the ballot box, but the politics of the knuckleduster.

Throughout 1922, Hitler's speeches were consistently 'for Germany' and 'against' democratic government. Rumours also circulated which indicated Hitler was preparing to launch a 'putsch' in Munich, to be followed by a 'march on Berlin' to crush German democratic government. In October 1922, Hitler persuaded members of the German Socialist Party (DSP), a similar 'national-socialist' style party based in Franconia in northern Bavaria, to join the Nazi Party, thus increasing party membership to 20,000. Hitler also had success in gaining sympathisers to the Nazi cause from several similar *Volkisch* groups in northern Germany, particularly in the Berlin area.

Mussolini's successful 'march on Rome' in October 1922, and the successful fascist seizure of power in Italy which followed it, raised the spirits of nationalist groups in Germany. Before Mussolini seized power in Italy, Hitler always referred to himself in speeches as the 'drummer' of the revolt against democracy, not a future German 'dictator'. He gave the impression, especially to leading figures in the army and members of the Bavarian upper classes, that he would use his party and his speaking talent to serve the greater cause of a German counter-revolution against Weimar democracy in a subordinate role. After October 1922, however, Hitler started to believe he might be the 'dynamic leader' needed to lead Germany out of the perceived mire. Significantly, Nazi propaganda began to develop the cult of Hitler as 'Germany's Mussolini'. The comparison between the 'leaderless democracy' of the Weimar Republic and a Germany led by a 'great leader', determined to restore German pride and power, now became a central feature of Nazi propaganda. In December 1922, the *Völkischer Beobachter*, which had not previously depicted Hitler as a future German leader, now started, little by little, to suggest Hitler was the 'heroic' leader Germany needed.

THE MUNICH BEER HALL PUTSCH

During 1923, Hitler's speeches, which reached larger and larger audiences, emphasised the need for a 'strong man to rescue Germany'. Most Nazis, supported by the other nationalist groups, convinced themselves an armed insurrection in Bavaria could lead to the toppling of the Weimar Republic. The major consequence of these ideas was the Munich Beer Hall Putsch of November 1923, a bungled attempt led by Adolf Hitler to lead a 'march to Berlin', with the aim of toppling Weimar democracy.

The Munich Beer Hall Putsch grew out of a broad-based Bavarian nationalist conspiracy, which emerged during the crisis year of 1923 when hyperinflation brought Germany to the verge of economic collapse, and French troops occupied the industrial Ruhr in a futile attempt to extract reparations payments from the German government. These events created a tangible atmosphere of crisis that put great strain on the existing democratic order. Most of the democratic parties, supported by the majority of nationalists, took part in the 'passive resistance' against the French occupation of the Ruhr. In a surprising move, Hitler opposed the policy of passive resistance, out of fear that opposition to France might encourage unity towards the existing German democratic government. 'Not down with France', Hitler said in a speech during the crisis, 'but down with the traitors to the Fatherland, down with the November criminals: that must be our slogan' (Fest, 1974: 164). Hitler's decision not to oppose the French occupation of the Ruhr prompted one leading Munich newspaper editorial to suggest the Nazi leader 'no longer captures the imagination of the German people' (ibid.: 171). It is, indeed, hard to fathom why Hitler, always attentive to the popular nationalist mood, chose to take a stand which was so out of step with it on this occasion. It seems Hitler, keen to topple Weimar democracy, was reluctant to throw his weight behind any cause that would strengthen it.

Meanwhile, the conspiracy to topple the Weimar Republic gathered momentum and supporters throughout Bavaria. Giving support to the conspiracy were: Hitler and the Nazi Party; leading figures within the local Bavarian command of the army (the *Reichswehr*); the *Kampfbund*, a para-military militant association; some well-known military heroes from the Great War, most notably General Ludendorff; and some prominent figures in the local police force, the Bavarian parliament, and an assortment of people in business and the local aristocracy. Taken as a whole, it was a powerful coalition of right-wing forces in Bavaria, provided they all stood together. In August 1923, a plan to overthrow the republic had begun to take concrete shape. The aim was to overthrow the Weimar government, and to establish an authoritarian nationalist regime which would allow Bavaria complete autonomy. Stores of weapons, munitions and transport vehicles were collected together in preparation for what was seen as an inevitable showdown with central government. Following a pre-arranged signal from the leaders of the Bavarian government, a strong force of heavily armed conspirators, including units from the army, the *Kampfbund* and the leaders of far-right groups, with Hitler in the vanguard, would march north to the German capital with the aim of seizing power. The conspiracy was given fresh impetus on 26 September 1923 when Gustav von Kahr, one of its firm supporters, was appointed state commissioner in Bavaria with 'dictatorial powers'. In this role, Kahr put Bavaria on a collision course with the Berlin government by refusing to proclaim a 'state of emergency' as he was requested to do by President Ebert under Article 48 of the Weimar constitution, and then by turning down a government request to ban the *Völkischer Beobachter*.

At the end of October 1923, the tactical details of the Bavarian conspiracy plan to overthrow the government were finalised by Kahr and his co-conspirators. In the early days of November 1923, however, some of the leading conspirators in the Bavarian government and the army started to have second thoughts, primarily because key figures in the army high command in Berlin told the Bavarian army conspirators they would defend the elected German government. On 3 November, General Otto von Lossow, the commander of the German army in Munich, advised Kahr that any march on Berlin would be futile. On 6 November, Kahr told representatives of the leading paramilitary organisations that the Bavarian government, the army and the police would not support independent action designed to bring down the state. After hearing this, Hitler sought a meeting with Kahr, who refused to meet him.

Hitler had staked his whole political career on the conspiracy going ahead. The trigger-happy right-wing paramilitary groups whose support Hitler had assiduously nurtured for most of the year wanted action. In the end, Hitler, unclear about whether Kahr would go ahead or not, decided abandoning the project so late in the day would be a humiliation from which his own political reputation was unlikely to recover. So he decided to press on with what now seemed a hopeless enterprise.

On 8 November, Kahr was due to address an audience of prominent Munich government officials and businessmen in a large beer hall (the Bürgerbräukeller) in the centre of Munich. Hitler suspected – quite wrongly – that Kahr intended to use the occasion to announce his own 'march on Berlin'. In fact, Kahr and his supporters had already abandoned the whole project, and kept Hitler in the dark about their decision. At 8.30 p.m. Hitler, accompanied by armed SA men, entered the Bürgerbräukeller while Kahr was in the midst of his speech. Hitler jumped on a chair or table (according to whose account you believe), then fired a single bullet from his revolver into the ceiling. He then walked towards the platform and announced that the National Revolution had begun and a new 'provisional' Reich government had been formed [*Doc. 6*]. Of course, this was a big lie: all Hitler had captured – and not for very long – was a large Munich beer hall. Kahr was led at pistol point by Hitler, accompanied by Colonel Hans von Seisser, head of the Bavarian state police, and Lossow, towards a small anteroom to discuss the 'national revolution'. Kahr found it difficult to take the whole matter seriously. Hitler offered him the post of regent of Bavaria, but the experienced local politician replied: 'Herr Hitler, you can have me shot or shoot me yourself. Whether I die is of no matter' (Shirer, 1961: 96). Hitler – beginning to realise that everything was not going according to plan – asked an SA man to go and collect General Ludendorff by car and bring him to the beer hall in the hope that his exalted presence might encourage Kahr to change his mind. When Ludendorff did arrive, about half an hour later, he told Kahr he supported Hitler. This appears to have impressed Kahr to some extent. However, Ludendorff was surprised to learn from the Nazi leader that in the new and fictional German government he had been assigned the post of commander of the army, and Hitler had appointed himself 'dictator of Germany'.

What happened next on this farcical evening is a matter of some dispute. Hitler claimed at his later trial that Kahr, Seisser and Lossow all agreed to join the conspiracy. Some of those present on the evening stated that Kahr did return to the platform after speaking with Hitler and Ludendorff, and announced he would support 'Hitler's Putsch' [*Doc. 6*]. It seems Kahr only did this because he was forced to at gunpoint. Kahr, Seisser and Lossow later said they all intended to suppress the revolt as soon as they were free to do so. What they did not say, of course, was that they had been plotting a conspiracy against the Berlin government themselves for many months and had only abandoned the project at the eleventh hour. Ludendorff claimed he knew nothing of what Hitler intended to do at the beer hall, and was taken by surprise by Hitler's impetuous action. Of course, he also omitted to say he had been conspiring with Hitler for months.

Hitler finally left the beer hall at 10.30 p.m. to go and calm down a clash between an SA paramilitary unit and troops which had erupted at the local barracks of the Army Engineers a few miles away. Once Hitler departed, so did Kahr, Seisser and Lossow. Kahr quickly took measures to strangle the rebellion at birth. He moved the Bavarian government to Regensburg, then issued a proclamation, fly-posted by the police throughout the Munich area, which claimed his earlier support for Hitler had been given at gunpoint. At the same time, he announced the Nazi Party and the paramilitary *Kampfbund* were now banned organisations. In the meantime, the Nazis had not taken control of a single army barracks or any important government building.

A few minutes before midnight, Hitler accepted his attempt to overthrow Weimar democracy had failed miserably, primarily because his supposed partners in the enterprise were not willing to support him. During the night, Hitler appeared totally clueless as to what to do next. After all, he had planned a putsch against the despised Berlin government, not his right-wing friends in the Bavarian government and his former paymasters in the local army. As a final gesture, he agreed – after some persuasion – to lead a demonstration through Munich (which took place on 9 November) in the vague hope this show of strength would miraculously rouse the army belatedly to support a 'march to Berlin'. 'If it comes off, all's well', Hitler told a close confidante, 'if not, we'll hang ourselves' (Fest, 1974: 187). Hitler led the demonstration, wearing his trademark shabby raincoat, along with the hapless Ludendorff, who had remained loyal to him, and a group of about 2000 Nazis (including 300 armed SA men). The group intended to march to the War Ministry building and seize it, but, as they reached a street leading to the Odeonplatz, the marchers found the route blocked by an armed police cordon. Several shots were then fired by both sides. At the end of this exchange, which lasted less than two minutes, fourteen members of the Nazi group and four policemen were dead, while others lay wounded. In the middle of the mayhem, Hitler fell awkwardly to the ground, dislocating his shoulder on landing. After getting to his feet, he ran away from the scene, leaving the dead and dying behind, and escaped in an ambulance. He later claimed – rather unconvincingly – that he had left so quickly because he thought Ludendorff had been killed, which was surely a reason for him to stay. Some years later, he concocted another story – also untrue – that he had bravely carried a child away from the scene to a waiting ambulance. In reality, Hitler's nerve failed him at the vital moment. When it was all over, Hitler turned up at the Munich house of a close friend, Ernst 'Putzi' Hanfstangl, a wealthy local landowner, where he was arrested by the police and taken to Landsberg prison on 11 November, to await trial on a charge of treason.

The Munich Beer Hall Putsch, the most significant event in the early history of the Nazi Party, was a hurriedly planned, bungled and humiliating failure. It failed because Hitler had allowed the Nazi Party to become a paramilitary organisation during 1923, and to become subsumed inside a conspiracy involving many disparate elements of the Bavarian right over which he had no control, and precious little significant influence. Although Hitler has been viewed as the instigator of the conspiracy to overthrow the German state in 1923, the reality was very different. It was really the Bavarian right, composed of the Bavarian government, the local army command and the state police, that had flirted with the idea of a putsch against the Berlin government, and it was they who decided, very late in the day, to abandon the project once they realised it had no support from the army high command in Berlin. Hitler, who had never been taken into the heart of the conspiracy, had meanwhile whipped up his own supporters into a frenzy, only to find he had already been deserted by his co-conspirators before he ever arrived at the Bürgerbräukeller. To make matters worse, they did not consider him important enough to even inform him of their change of heart. Hitler felt he could not retreat without damaging his own claim to be the leading 'revolutionary' against Weimar democracy, so he pressed on towards humiliating failure. In the early days of November 1923, therefore, it seemed Adolf Hitler's brief but extremely colourful political career had come to an abrupt and untimely end.

CHAPTER FOUR

THE IDEOLOGY OF HITLER AND THE NAZI PARTY

Nazism was a vague, eclectic, rag bag ideology which drew on a wide variety of sources. It lacked the coherent, systematic economic foundations of Marxist–Leninist communism. It is even difficult to determine whether it was 'progressive' or 'backward looking'. Unlike Marxism, which aimed to destroy the existing economic and political system, Nazism was much more willing to collaborate with existing power structures, and to follow seemingly backward-looking ideas in pursuit of its objectives. Nazism also lacked the ideological backing and intellectual weight of a Karl Marx. In essence, Nazism was a rather ill-thought-out 'third way' between liberal democracy and communism. It grew at a time when mass democracy was being introduced in Germany for the first time and when the world economic system was greatly strained by the consequences of the First World War.

Nazism built its support by tapping into the negative feelings of certain sections of German society towards such things as the 'harsh' terms of the Versailles treaty, high inflation, the instability of democratic government, the economic position of Jews in German society and the growth of a vibrant communist movement. Nazi ideology pointed to the 'enemies' inside Germany: communists, socialists, trade unionists, democrats and Jews, and then suggested that the elimination of these groups from positions of power could only be achieved through a 'National Socialist Revolution' that would establish a strong state, led by a strong leader, who was determined to rebuild military power, shake off Versailles and make Germany, once and for all, the most dominant power in the world.

LINKS WITH FASCISM AND TOTALITARIANISM

Although Nazism had many unique characteristics, there has always been a tendency to bracket it under the general label of 'fascism', a term which invokes words such as 'violent', 'repressive' and 'dictatorial'. However, finding a general definition of fascism has proved extremely difficult. For a start, there was no great philosopher who codified fascist ideology. This is hardly surprising given that fascism prided itself on being anti-intellectual and opposed to 'rational' thought. It is not surprising, therefore, to discover that the statements and writings of the leading supporters of fascism are as dense as fog [*Doc.* 8]. The incoherence and anti-intellectual nature of fascism reflected the narrowness of the minds that supported it. The only explanation Mussolini, the Italian fascist leader, ever offered of the ideological basis of fascism was a short article published in an Italian encyclopedia, in which he defined a fascist as a fervent patriot for whom the preservation of the state is most crucial. To Marxists, the strident, uncritical, patriotic loyalty fascists expressed towards a powerful state was merely a 'bourgeois device' used by upper-class reactionary groups who wanted to crush mass democracy, communism and the growing labour movement in one fell swoop in order to safeguard their own threatened position at the top of society. This view is reinforced by the fact that authoritarian dictatorships in Germany and Italy were established through the existing legal and administrative machinery of these states, and supported by many upper-class elite groups in the army, civil service and big business.

A more sophisticated version of the idea of fascism being a sort of 'elite conspiracy' to crush communism and democracy was offered by the leading Italian Marxist writer Antonio Gramsci (who was executed by the fascists). He suggested that capitalism – especially in Europe – was going through a severe crisis in the early part of the twentieth century, in which the dominant classes of the nineteenth century were finding it increasingly difficult to manipulate the mass of the population to support their rule and were concerned that communism might sweep them away in a tidal wave of revolution. In these circumstances, fascism became the repressive means of restoring these classes' hegemony over society by offering the masses a seemingly popular form of rule, led by a dominant individual, when in reality this was merely a vehicle for destroying the threatening power of communism and the egalitarian principles of mass democracy. Of course, the problem with this view of fascism is that it attaches very little importance to the popularity of fascism among certain sections of German and Italian society, which, on this view, were manipulated.

Seymour Lipset, in his influential study *Political Man*, viewed fascism in a rather different way, portraying it as a genuine 'revolt of the middle classes' who felt trapped between the growth of big business and the revolutionary politics of the workers and thought the liberal democratic parties could not haul them out of the mounting economic distress after 1918 or restore the stability and order they so desired. On this view, fascism had a genuine appeal to these groups and was not simply imposed upon them from above through manipulation (Payne, 1995: 349). However,

Lipset's interpretation, which concentrated on the German case alone, has been challenged by many studies of voting behaviour in Germany between 1918 and 1933, which have shown that the Nazi Party did not just gain votes from disaffected liberals, but drew the bulk of its support from small right-wing nationalist fringe parties, from prosperous members of the upper middle class, and from a significant number of voters in rural areas who had previously not voted for any other party (Fischer, 1995).

The problem of finding a general theory to explain 'fascism' is further complicated by the development of the concept of totalitarianism, which argues that communist and fascist dictatorships in power were different sides of the same coin. Carl Friedrich, for example, put forward a 'six point' test to evaluate a 'totalitarian' regime, consisting of: an official ideology, a single mass party, a terrorist police force, monopoly control of the media, a monopoly of arms, and central control of the economy. Totalitarian regimes of the communist or fascist variety made the masses conform to their rule or face dire consequences. The main problem with the totalitarian model is that it is a rather static model which views communist and fascist regimes as basically similar, thus downplaying the actual ideological differences and aims of Nazism in Germany and Bolshevism in the Soviet Union and failing to see the real economic differences and class relationships within each society.

The acceptance of a general theory of fascism has also encountered problems in gaining credibility among historians and political scientists. No single theory of fascism can possibly explain the different characteristics of the many different regimes and political parties which called themselves fascist and operated throughout Europe during the inter-war period. Even Nazism and Italian fascism exhibited major ideological differences. Race was of fundamental significance in Nazi ideology, but of comparative insignificance to Italian fascists. Mussolini gave open support to many aspects of modernity, while Hitler tended to stress the need to incorporate many lost medieval customs into German society. At the same time, there were many similarities between Italian fascism and National Socialism, including extreme nationalism, emphasis on strong dictatorial leadership, a strong anti-Marxism (which implied the destruction of working-class and Marxist organisations), ruthless repression of all opposition groups, contempt for democratic forms of government, the glorification of war, strong support for rearmament, a stress on the need for economic self-sufficiency, the use of propaganda, and, especially in the rise to power of Mussolini and Hitler, the forging of alliances with existing anti-democratic elites within the state, and the creation of paramilitary organisations of ex-soldiers to add to the sense of general chaos on the streets. In most respects, fascist ideology opposed existing 'established' religion, but at the same time it projected a messianic mission, which resembled a devotion to a religious faith. Fascism was a sort of political religion, one which expressed a rather utopian vision of the future, in which a new state and a 'new man' would prosper. Fascism also stressed action and daring, which appealed to young people. Another key characteristic of Fascist ideology was its stress on male chauvinism and male domination over society; Fascist ideology had little interest in women's equality or female rights.

In spite of the similarities between the Italian and German versions of fascism, many historians do not accept that Nazism was simply a derivative version of Italian fascism, primarily because the differences between Italian fascism and National Socialism, when examined in detail, outweigh the similarities, especially the overarching race theory within National Socialism, to which all other aspects of Nazi ideology and policy were inextricably linked. Put this way, Nazism can be viewed as a unique phenomenon because its emphasis on race, and the anti-modern idea of the *Volkisch* state, differed greatly from the modernist ideas of Italian fascism. More importantly, Hitler's unique personality and ideological obsession with race gave Nazism specific German–Austrian characteristics which must be analysed in the context of the historical development of Germany.

THE HISTORICAL ROOTS OF NAZISM

No major historical force emerges without some prior development, and the historical roots of Nazism stretch back into history. Nazi propaganda certainly acknowledged its debt to many past influences. Hitler claimed: 'A man who has no sense of history is like a man who has no eyes and ears' (Bullock, 1962: 397). A famous Nazi postcard, very popular in the period, featured Hitler's head alongside those of Frederick the Great, Bismarck and Hindenburg. Hitler also frequently claimed that the Third Reich represented continuity with the First Reich (the medieval Holy Roman Empire) and the Second Reich (established by Bismarck and ended by the 1919 peace settlement). Even in his bunker, right up until his suicide, Hitler kept a portrait of Frederick the Great, the eighteenth-century soldier-king, on a bedside table.

Some historians have suggested that Germany followed a special and unique historical path (*Sonderweg*), which glorified authoritarian rule, war and territorial conquest. National Socialism was a logical consequence of these German preoccupations. Many of Hitler's supposedly 'unique' foreign policy aims turn out, on closer inspection, not to have been so novel after all. The concept of *Lebensraum*, the acquisition of living space, not only had precedents in German history, but was mentioned frequently in most of the pre-1914 Pan-German League pamphlets. German dominance of eastern Europe – and the subordination of the Slavs – were key aims not only of Frederick the Great in the eighteenth century but also of the Kaiser during the First World War. Most conservative nationalist groups in Germany, even in the Weimar period, advocated most of Hitler's foreign policy aims. On the other hand, many other historians have suggested Nazism had no deep roots in German history. Nationalism, anti-Semitism and social Darwinism, all regarded as key influences on Nazism, were actually ideas imported from outside Germany. A policy of systematic killing aimed at the Jewish population had no precedent in pre-1914 German policy.

It is, in fact, possible to view Nazism as a unique German response to specific problems thrown up by the First World War: as a reaction against modern and urbanised industrial society; a reaction against rapid techno-logical change and innovation; a reaction against the growth of socialism and mass democracy; a response to the development of mass society; a response to deep economic problems, most notably high inflation; and a desire to restore confidence in a defeated nation. It is very difficult to isolate the long-term historical influences on the development of Nazism from the particular characteristics of the period in which it gained prominence.

THE PHILOSOPHICAL ROOTS OF NATIONAL SOCIALISM

Attempting to isolate the philosophical roots of National Socialism is equally difficult. A great deal of ink has been spilled trying to explain where Hitler got his ideas from. Although he was an avid reader, he did not read philosophical tracts in depth – and regarding him as some sort of ideo-logical guru is quite absurd. Many of Hitler's ideas – especially in the period after the First World War – were borrowed from some of the leading members of the party. One important figure who influenced Hitler in the early days of the party in Munich was Dietrich Eckart, a poet, playwright and journalist whose best friend was a wine glass. Hitler described Eckart – a serious alcoholic – as 'a fatherly friend'. He claimed to have been greatly influenced by Eckart's second-hand nationalist and anti-Semitic ideas. Eckart was very fond of telling his fellow Nazi members to 'keep your blood pure', even though his own was always somewhat heavily diluted by alcohol. Eckart was the author of several early Nazi pamphlets from which Hitler undoubtedly drew inspiration, including a bitter attack on 'the Jews' entitled *That is the Jew*, which argued that the restoration of the German *Volk* could only be achieved through the 'removal of the Jewish menace' (Zalampas, 1989: 37). Eckart's virulent anti-Semitism, and his flaky eugenic theories concerning race, had a profound influence on Hitler's own ideas on these subjects. It seems that word-of-mouth ideas, received second-hand, exerted a greater impact on Hitler's ideas than any deep reading of philosophy.

While in the Landsberg fortress, Hitler claimed he read works by Nietzsche, Hegel, Houston Stewart Chamberlain and Treitschke, even though those present at the time later claimed he rarely read such works in any detail. Nevertheless, it is possible to detect Hegel's view of the state having 'supreme power over the individual' in Hitler's writings and speeches. Heinrich von Treitschke, the German historian, did influence Hitler, in particular his view that 'war is the highest expression of man'. There is also little doubt that the work of Nietzsche, however assimilated, penetrated into Hitler's thinking. Nietzsche was a nineteenth-century German philosopher who was deeply disturbed by the dizzy pace of European social and industrial change. He predicted modern society would result in 'the death of God'. What Hitler latched on to in Nietzsche's writings were his fervent criticisms of democratic forms of government, his praise of violence and war, and his prediction of the emergence of the coming 'master race' led by an all-powerful 'superman', supported by a small elite, who together would 'rule the world'. The term 'Lords of the Earth', coined by Nietzsche, is constantly used throughout *Mein Kampf* and was repeatedly mentioned by Hitler – and most leading Nazis – during the era of the Third Reich. Nietzsche was certainly treated as a deep philosophical influence on National Socialism during the Nazi era, even if the nuances of his philosophy were way beyond the bar-room logic of most Nazis. There is equally little doubt that Hitler viewed himself as a 'superman', who had been marked out by 'providence' to lead Germany to the pinnacle of world power.

Hitler was very clearly attracted by the idea of the 'survival of the fittest', and a crude social Darwinism permeates a great deal of Hitler's writings and speeches. By the late nineteenth century, and in the early twentieth century, social Darwinistic ideas, derived largely from anthropological and zoological research, were extremely fashionable in Germany and Austria, and throughout most of western Europe. Such theories tended to reinforce the appeal of nationalism, especially in Germany and Austria. Hitler did believe life was a 'struggle between strength and weakness' in which only the strong would prevail, through the use of superior force. Although such ideas were influenced by the writings of Charles Darwin, there is no evidence Hitler ever read any of his work in the original. Even so, Hitler was unquestionably a social Darwinist, and this had a key ideological influence upon his ideas.

Closely related to social Darwinistic thinking were ideas about race, which was another crucial aspect of Nazi ideology. Modern concepts of discriminatory racism were postulated during the eighteenth-century Enlightenment, in the writings of leading European geographers and anthropologists, but they grew more well known from the mid-nineteenth century. The thinker whose work greatly influenced future writers on race was Comte Arthur de Gobineau, who divided humanity into three basic races – white, yellow and black – and who put forward the view that race was the key to the development of history. Gobineau argued that all higher forms of civilisation had flowed from the superior white race, and that the highest form of that race was the 'Aryan', the highest human species of all. According to Gobineau, the purity of the Aryan race had decayed over centuries due to racial mixing with 'inferior races'. The only means of creating a future master race, thought Gobineau, was to ensure that 'Aryans' only produced children in union with other 'Aryans'. Yet he was pessimistic about whether this could ever be achieved.

Other racial theorists rejected the pessimism in Gobineau's writings and called instead for eugenic policies to defend the so-called 'higher races'. Such ideas on race soon became popular in many parts of Europe and were particularly extensive throughout German-speaking central Europe. The greatest populariser of racist ideas in Germany and Austria was an eccentric Englishman who had settled in Germany: Houston Stewart Chamberlain, who was a leading figure in the German branch of the Gobineau Society. His famous book *Foundations of the Nineteenth Century* (1899) became extremely popular with Pan-German groups in Germany, and provided the Nazis with the basis of their master race ideas. Chamberlain promoted the idea in Germany and Austria that the key driving force in historical development was race. At the top of the racial pyramid was the 'Teuton' ('the soul of our culture'), whose highest form was the 'tall, blond, blue-eyed, magnificent Aryan' which was found in its 'purest form' in Germany. It was through the development of the Aryan that Germans could become the 'masters of the earth'. There is little doubt that, in Germany and Austria, the rapid growth in popularity of racial doctrines which eulogised the Aryan was always accompanied by anti-Semitism.

Another important influence on Hitler's ideas were the musical operatic works and political views of Richard Wagner. Hitler often claimed that anyone wanting to understand National Socialism fully 'must know Wagner'. He harboured a strong dislike of the Jews, and he venerated German nationalism in many of his operas (Shirer, 1961: 133). What particularly attracted Hitler to Wagner were his vividly staged operas which pitted German medieval heroes with tribal codes in a struggle against their enemies. In a very real sense, Nazism was not just about ideas – it was about putting ideas into action. Hitler viewed Nazi Germany as the enactment of some great real life theatrical opera, and the vast Nazi displays of pomp and ceremony, which characterised so much of the ceremonial life of the Nazi Party, owed a great deal to the inspiration of the operas of Wagner. Indeed, the end of *Götterdämmerung*, when Wotan, the leading character, sets on fire Valhalla, has great similarities to Hitler's flame-filled hell in Berlin at the end of the Second World War.

What these ideas on race tended to reinforce was a strong form of defensive nationalism. There is little doubt that the intense feelings of nationalism that existed in Germany, Austria and among the upper classes throughout European society in the early part of the twentieth century were linked to fears about the consequences of the growth of internationalism, and especially the growing popularity of the anti-nationalist creed of Marxism. Though right-wing nationalist groups did not appeal for support to nationalism alone, it was a key aspect of their ideological thinking. Hence, Nazism can be viewed as a reactionary response to the growth of socialist forces, mass democracy and modern urban industrial society. Nazism sought to recapture the revolutionary potential of nationalism, which had first come to prominence during the era of the French revolution.

HITLER'S CENTRAL ROLE IN NAZI IDEOLOGY

Of course, the key to understanding the essence of Nazism does not lie only in isolating the various influences on National Socialism, but in grasping how these ideas were assimilated into Nazi ideology by Adolf Hitler. The major source for comprehending Nazi ideology is *Mein Kampf* (*My Struggle*), written by Hitler and published in two volumes, the first of which appeared in July 1925, the second in December 1926. The original title, 'Four and a Half Years of Battle Against Lies, Stupidity and Cowardice: Account Settled', was rejected as too long-winded by Max Amann, Hitler's publishing manager. *Mein Kampf* is part autobiography, part ideological tract, and part blueprint for political action. It is not a great work of political theory, running to 752 pages – in its original form – of verbose, subjective and repetitious prose which reads like the extended ranting of an extremely prejudiced person. In spite of these obvious weaknesses, *Mein Kampf* remains a very important book for understanding the essence of Nazi ideology because it outlines the most complete presentation of the fundamental principles of Hitler's *Weltanschauung* ('world view', or ideology), the techniques of Nazi propaganda, the plan for destroying Marxism and eliminating Jews from German society, the concept and policies of a future National Socialist state and Hitler's central foreign policy objectives. Between 1925 and 1945, *Mein Kampf* sold 10 million copies and was translated into sixteen languages. It made Hitler a very rich man and the world a poorer place.

THE IMPORTANCE OF FOREIGN POLICY

The central foreign policy aim of Nazism was to make Germany the most dominant power in Europe, and to gain revenge for the German defeat in the First World War. As a result, the largest amount of space in *Mein Kampf* is concerned with the aims of German foreign policy under Hitler's rule.

Hitler's first objective was to 'abolish the Treaty of Versailles'. To achieve this, he intended to revise the treaty by unilateral acts when suitable opportunities arose. If Hitler's foreign policy objectives had been merely limited to revising Versailles, the course of German history would have been very different, and Hitler would now be judged as one of the most successful German leaders in history. However, doing away with the 'hated' Versailles treaty was for Hitler just the essential prelude to a resurgence of German militarism of a more extreme variety than had existed before. 'To demand that the 1914 frontiers of Germany be restored', wrote Hitler in *Mein Kampf*, 'is a political absurdity'. In fact, Hitler – although often accused of being a counter-revolutionary – was deeply critical of pre-1914 German foreign policy, especially the aim of seeking a colonial empire outside Europe – the so-called 'World Policy' – and engaging in a wasteful naval rivalry with Britain. Instead, Hitler intended to concentrate his own territorial aims exclusively on the European continent. To begin with, he would incorporate all German speakers in Austria, the Sudetenland and Poland into a greater German Reich. Hitler knew these territorial acquisitions would meet with opposition from the French government. Hence, a war with France – 'the inexorable enemy of the German people' – was always implicit in Hitler's foreign policy thinking. As a counterweight to French hostility to German aims in Europe, he wanted to build close relations with Britain, thereby avoiding the severe Anglo-German antagonism that had characterised relations between the two countries in the years which led to the outbreak of the First World War. Indeed, Hitler hoped to persuade the British government to abandon its long-standing support for upholding a balance of power in Europe, and enter an alliance with Germany under whose terms the British Empire would be guaranteed in return for Britain allowing Germany a 'free hand' to gain territory in eastern Europe without interference.

The major aim of Hitler's foreign policy – closely linked to his racial ideas – was to gain *Lebensraum* (living space) for Germany in eastern Europe through a war of conquest against the Soviet Union. According to Hitler:

> If land is desired in Europe, it could be obtained by and large only at the expense of the Soviet Union, and this meant the new Reich must set itself on the march along the road of the Teutonic Knights of old, to obtain by the German sword, sod for the German plough and daily bread for the nation.

The aim of *Lebensraum* was to defeat the Soviet Union in war, providing enough living space to assure German 'freedom of existence' and paving the way for a German population explosion in the newly acquired areas. The eventual aim was to create a Greater German Reich of 250 million 'racially pure' Germans completely self-sufficient in food and raw materials. In Hitler's view, the task of gaining *Lebensraum* in the east had been made easier for the German army by the Russian Revolution which had 'handed over Russia to the Jews' and thereby weakened its military prowess. The war of conquest against the Soviet Union was, for Hitler, not only a clear and concrete aim, but also a crusade to rid eastern Europe of his two most hated enemies: Bolsheviks and Jews.

Of course, the concept of *Lebensraum* did not originate with Hitler. It was a term used by many groups on the right of German politics in the Weimar period. The idea featured very strongly in pre-1914 Pan-German League pamphlets, many of which we know were read by Hitler during his Vienna period. It appears to have been used interchangeably by those right-wing groups which desired a unification of all 'German speakers' (*Volksdeutsche*) who were scattered throughout eastern Europe and those groups (such as the Nazi Party) which used the concept to justify support for vast territorial conquest for Germany in eastern Europe, primarily at the expense of the Soviet Union. At the root of the concept was the idea of Germans not having enough land to live on, thereby reducing Germany's ability to become a dominant world power. The central aim of the future National Socialist state was to prepare the German people for a war of conquest in eastern Europe to gain *Lebensraum* at the expense of the Soviet Union.

THE CENTRALITY OF RACE

At the centre of Nazi ideology, and its dominant theoretical factor, was race. Hitler was not, as is often routinely argued, a mere 'German nationalist'. He often conceded – mostly in private – that the concept of the 'Aryan' race extended to many other people in central Europe, and even to England, to some 'Aryan' people throughout Europe and to Anglo-Saxons in the USA. Such revolutionary ideas, which became more apparent during the Second World War, would have frightened many Germans and weakened the appeal of Nazism before 1933, so Hitler kept quiet about them.

Hitler viewed all of human history not as a class struggle, but as a struggle for existence between strong and pure races over weak and mixed ones. War ('that great purifier') was viewed by Hitler as the means by which the strongest and purest race would dominate the weak. The question as to how Germans would become the strongest race on earth occupied a great deal of Hitler's attention in *Mein Kampf*. Hitler divided the world into three racial groups: (i) 'Aryans' – defined as those races who created cultures; (ii) the 'bearers of culture' – classed as those races who cannot create culture, but who can copy from Aryans; and (iii) 'inferior peoples' – defined as those who have no capacity to create culture, or to copy from others, but can only destroy cultures. The key objective of Hitler's racial policy, therefore, was to create a racially pure 'Aryan' folk community (*Volksgemeinschaft*) of Germans, which, due to its alleged superiority, would have the right to subjugate 'inferior' peoples (Geary, 1993).

THE FUNCTION OF ANTI-SEMITISM AND ANTI-MARXISM IN NAZI IDEOLOGY

If the Aryan possessed all the positive qualities Hitler admired, the opposite was true of Hitler's two most hated enemies: Marxists and Jews. Hitler regarded the Marxist desire to foment a 'class war' as the chief threat to the unity of the nation. A virulent hatred of Marxism – and everything associated with it – runs through all of Hitler's writings and speeches [*Doc. 11*]. At the core of Hitler's ideological mission was a desire to eliminate Marxism within Germany, and then to exterminate Bolshevism during a war against the Soviet Union. At his trial for treason in March 1924, Hitler told the court he wanted to be 'the breaker of Marxism', and elsewhere he frequently spoke of his desire to 'annihilate' Marxism.

Hitler's anti-Marxism was interwoven with a virulent anti-Semitism. Whenever Hitler spoke of Marxists, he implied they were either 'Jews' or 'controlled by Jews'. Hitler defined 'the Jews' not as a religious group, but as a united race who were planning 'a world conspiracy' to undermine national unity. This far-fetched conspiracy was supposedly outlined in *The Protocols of Zion*, a forged document which was circulated widely in Germany before 1914 and outlined a Zionist plan for Jewish world domination. Hitler believed that, because Jews were a 'stateless people' (the state of Israel was not established until 1947), they sought to undermine the 'ethnic unity' and 'racial purity' of every state they inhabited. Hitler ascribed every ill in the world to 'Jewish influence'.

Anti-Semitism had two functions within Nazi ideology: it provided a very simple explanation for all the divisions and problems in German society, and suggested a full solution to those ills could only be achieved by 'eliminating' Jews from German society. In Nazi ideology, 'the Jew' was a universal scapegoat, responsible for Marxism, democracy, internationalism, pacifism, class war, freedom of the press, prostitution, venereal disease, modernism in art, and much else. Behind every anti-patriotic, disunifying force lay, according to Hitler, 'the eternal Jew', plotting and scheming to weaken the 'blood purity' and will of the Aryan race. Once again, the extreme radical nature of Hitler's anti-Semitism was toned down greatly, especially in the critical period 1928 to 1933 when Nazi voting strength was increasing. In reality, Hitler's anti-Semitism was demonic in its passion and formed a central aspect of his ideological thinking. He never fully explained what he meant before 1933 about his desire to 'eliminate' the Jewish danger, but given his ideological mind-set there is little doubt he saw such an elimination as extermination, if he got the chance, especially on a pan-European scale.

THE FOLK COMMUNITY

When Hitler discussed the future shape of the Nazi state, he thought in terms of creating a popular folk (or ethnically unified) community, or *Volksgemeinschaft*, bound together by 'common blood' ties and guided by the will of an all-powerful leader. The idea of creating a folk community was a popular and nostalgic idea, supported by all sections of the German nationalist right. The German word *Volk* when translated into English is rendered usually as 'people', but in German it possessed a much deeper meaning, denoting an idealised return to a primitive rural form of ethnic unity based on 'blood and soil', with a romanticised (and often mytho-logised) view of Germany's medieval past and a strong belief that there was an ethnic and unique race, the Germans, which had a shared set of values, deep bonds and blood ties stretching back into the lost mist of time. *Volkisch* nationalism tended to stress the unique and distinct aspects of 'German' people, culture and even the landscape. Most *Volkisch* writers claimed German medieval society was one in which tribes were bound together by shared language, feelings of loyalty, blood ties and love of working on the soil. The authority in such a society was passed down from a leader, who exercised power for the benefit of the whole community. The economy was based on self-sufficiency, home production, and fair barter between kith and kin in a romanticised folk community. When war came, so the *Volkisch* myth suggested, the whole community would be united in a struggle for its own people. It was the creation of a modern industrial society that broke this unity by placing profits, productivity and trade above natural kindred bonds. Such attitudes tended to reject Christianity in favour of a mystical view of the past, the cosmos and the environment. Not surprisingly, the idea of the *Volk* tended to be opposed to industrialisation, individualism, urbanisation, class conflict and cosmopolitan ideas; a 'return to the soil' was idealised as the answer to these problems. The goal of supporters of these *Volkisch* ideals was a harmonious united society which idealised rural life.

The appeal of such ideas before 1914 was strongest among the lower middle classes – among traders and merchants and small-scale farmers – but some elements in the landed aristocratic class who also felt threatened by the rapid growth of industrialisation and the liberality of thought which accompanied it were also attracted by these ideas. Not surprisingly, *Volkisch* groups felt that all 'modern' influences were related to 'Jewish influence'. In pre-1914 German society, *Volkisch* groups were in a very small minority within the middle classes, with very limited representation in the Reichstag, usually in the form of small special interest parties with limited electoral support. What supporters of *Volkisch* ideas lacked before 1914 was a major political party championing these romantic ideals.

In the aftermath of the German defeat in the First World War, however, support for this nostalgic and utopian vision of a 'lost Germany' gathered in strength and was certainly a factor which pervaded Nazi ideology and helped to attract support for the Nazi Party from the middle classes as well as the rural community. Most supporters of the *Volkisch* myth wanted a return to a simpler, less complicated, greener society, based on principles such as hierarchy, patriotism, social harmony, order and obedience. The idea of the urban dweller being trapped by modernity was a very strong image in Nazi propaganda, which elevated a love of nature, the landscape and working on the land as the real means to a happy and contented life [*Doc. 14*]. The idea of creating a united national community in which individuals would unite in the service of the community, led by a powerful leader and supported by an elite (similar to the medieval Teutonic Knights), was at the centre of the Nazi appeal to the middle classes and to rural communities.

Hitler had a romanticised and utopian view of German culture, which he believed had been undermined by powerful 'non-German' forces. In Hitler's view, the rural and racial harmony between knights and peasants of medieval times had been destroyed by the rise of the bourgeoisie, the growth of industrial society, the rise of socialism and the influence of 'the Jews' in German society. The way forward, therefore, was to take Germany backward, to a simpler rural lifestyle in which each German could live on the land. The type of government needed by such a community would be an authoritarian one, with no majority decisions, no democratic votes, one where everything was decided 'by one man' and an 'elite of leaders'. The leader would give orders downwards, which he would expect to be obeyed. The individual in such a society would be expected to follow orders, without question or discussion. The future Nazi state would not promote equality, only equality of opportunity [*Doc. 10*]. Yet the individual who prospered would be expected to serve the 'common good', and be willing to be self-sacrificing in the service of the nation. Indeed, 'Common Good before Individual Good' was a key Nazi slogan. To the powerful *Volkisch* myth, Hitler added the idea of the front-line community (*Frontsgemein-schaft*), which consisted of the soldiers who had fought in a common struggle against the enemy in the First World War and who had been 'stabbed in the back' by socialists, war profiteers and Jews at home. Hitler attempted to suggest he would recreate the unity of the soldiers in the war in a German society under Nazi rule.

Hitler defined the folk community as a 'classless society' in which individuals would find their own 'natural level' through hard work, will-power and effort. Hitler did often speak of the entire German nation being of 'pure Aryan stock', but on closer inspection it is clear that Hitler felt it could be achieved by a process of selecting who should and should not have children in a Nazi-run society. The key aim was to get rid of all 'racial impurities' from German blood, thereby paving the way for a return to a *Volksgemeinschaft*, a 'blood pure' community of Germans living in harmony on the land. Yet Hitler believed that only a select group ('based on the aristocratic idea of nature'), meaning the stronger, the taller, the fitter and the faster, would become part of the Aryan elite. Those who did not match up to the Aryan ideal of perfection would have to content themselves with being loyal and patriotic members of the folk community. The Nazi elite were the nobility (the Teutonic Knights), the remainder were loyal peasants, and all were part of a united and contented folk community. In practice, Hitler was more pragmatic about *Volkisch* ideals than many of his followers. In his search for power, the anti-capitalist, anti-big business and anti-bourgeois aspects of Nazi ideology were downplayed, and it was 'Jews and Marxists' who became the chief and easy targets of Nazi abuse. Attacking 'the Jews' was easier than attempting to dismantle modern industrial society and returning Germans to the land.

In essence, Nazism wanted to create the conditions in which there would be equality of opportunity, but Hitler did not favour an equal society [*Doc. 11*]. It would be possible to reach the top in Hitler's society, not just with traditional academic qualifications but also with 'racial qualifications', which amounted to the ability to trace a long 'German' family tree, combined with the essential physical attributes of being blond, tall, fit and physically strong. The abilities of the 'self-made' businessman were also included in these criteria. Hitler promised the Nazi state would promote the 'victory of the better and the stronger', and demand the subordination of 'the inferior and the weaker'. German citizens were expected not to 'weaken' the 'purity of their blood' by having children with people of different races. If a racially pure, thoroughbred elite sort of German could be created, then Hitler believed it would be 'the highest species of humanity on this earth'. When Hitler spoke of 'race' and 'purity of blood', therefore, he was always thinking of the creation of a 'racial elite' (*Herrenvolk*) who would rule society. All Germans could aspire to be part of the 'master race', but in reality, Hitler realised, only a small proportion of Germans would be able to meet his exacting entry requirements. Outside the 'racial elite' in the proposed Nazi state were 'the masses'. Hitler spoke of 'nationalising the masses' through successful propaganda. He believed they could be duped into supporting just about any policy 'if the same message was repeated over and over again'. In Hitler's view the great mass of people 'will more easily fall victim to a great lie than to a small one'. It seems clear 'the masses' had the same position as a private soldier in Hitler's mind: they were to follow orders, without comment. They were to support the policies of the Nazi elite – without comment. They were to accept the unequal nature of Nazi society – without comment. Nazism was, therefore, fundamentally a doctrine of equality of opportunity but one which accepted it was bolstering and strengthening a very hierarchical and unequal society.

THE FUNCTION OF SOCIALISM IN NATIONAL SOCIALISM

This helps to explain why Hitler was always extremely vague about where 'socialism' came into his proposed folk community. The issue of exactly what Hitler meant by 'National Socialism' caused enormous divisions within the Nazi Party before 1933, and much confusion outside it [*Doc. 11*]. Hitler claimed that National Socialism was a 'dictatorship of the whole community'. It would aim to create a society in which there were no class barriers [*Doc. 12*].

The idea of National Socialism had been an open topic of discussion among extreme German nationalists for many years before the advent of the Nazi Party. In the 1890s a liberal pastor, Friedrich Naumann, set up a National-Social Association which aimed to persuade industrial workers – who might be attracted to real socialism – to give support to the existing state. The terms 'German Socialism' and 'National Socialism' were used interchangeably by members of anti-Marxist and anti-Semitic *Volkisch* groups in Germany and Austria. These groups attempted to stress that National Socialism was concerned with the strengthening of the nation, not narrow sectional interests.

Hitler favoured this concept of socialism over the egalitarian variety espoused by 'real' socialists. Hitler defined his odd brand of 'socialism' in the following way:

Whoever is prepared to make the national cause his own to such an extent that he knows no higher ideal than the welfare of his nation; whoever has understood our great national anthem, 'Deutschland über Alles', to mean that nothing in the wide world surpasses in his eyes this Germany, people and land – that man is a socialist.

On this definition, National Socialism was a form of uncritical loyalty to the state. The 'radical' wing of the Nazi Party, led by Gregor Strasser, argued that a National Socialist state should control the economic life and resources of the nation, and then use them for the benefit of the whole community. Hitler realised such ideas would alienate business and army support. As a result, 'socialist' ideas were marginalised in the Nazi programme before Hitler came to power – and most of the supporters of these ideas were brutally killed in the blood purge (known as the Night of the Long Knives) which took place in 1933.

As we have seen, much of Nazi ideology was borrowed from ideas long current in nationalist and anti-Semitic groups, which were themselves borrowed from the ideas of right-wing philosophers and social Darwinist writers. Nazism, like a very large sponge, soaked up these ideas, and then wrung them out to form the misty sludge known as National Socialism. Yet the importance of ideology for Hitler was not in the ideas themselves: most of them were mythologised and utopian dreams, unsuited to the practical realities of a modern industrial society, or were eugenic and racist mumbo jumbo which, if applied, would inevitably lead, even though the road might be twisted, towards genocide and war. Hitler could scarcely define either an 'Aryan' or a 'Jew', and he often admitted privately that most of his master race ideas had little chance of being achieved in his lifetime, if at all. What Nazi ideology could do successfully was to define – in exaggerated terms – both internal enemies – 'the Jews and the Marxists' – and external ones – France and the Soviet Union – all of which had to be 'destroyed' or 'eliminated' or 'exterminated' before the Germans could begin to create their *Volkisch* utopia. Yet in the period when Hitler rose to power, it was the optimistic and utopian dream of creating a harmonious *Volksgemein-schaft* of racially pure Aryans that struck the most responsive chord among those people who decided to vote for the Nazi Party. Such a utopian dream could only have prospered in the dark of a very black night.

CHAPTER FIVE

THE NAZI PARTY: ORGANISATION, PROPAGANDA AND MEMBERSHIP

The rapid growth in support for the Nazi Party is one of the most remarkable occurrences in political history. A great deal of credit for the rise of Nazism has been attributed to the leadership ability, hypnotic oratory and political flexibility of Adolf Hitler. But the 'Hitler factor' alone cannot fully explain why the Nazi Party went from a small fringe party based in Munich to the most popular party in Germany between 1919 and 1932. In order to comprehend why the Nazis were able to mount such a devastating challenge to the existing political order in Weimar Germany, we must also examine three important aspects of the Nazi Party: organisation, propaganda and membership.

ORGANISATION

The Nazi Party had a centralised, hierarchical, but very efficient organisation, whose nerve centre was in Munich. The party was organised on the *Führerprinzip* (leadership principle), which held that the decisions of the leader were binding on every official, branch and member of the party [*Doc. 5*]. The leader ('Führer') of the party enjoyed dictatorial power over all the administrative and organisational functions of the party. He delegated power to individuals in return for complete loyalty to his leadership. Hitler had the right to hire and fire all the party's leading officials, and could even expel any individual party member. The leader also chose candidates at elections, and appointed all the leading officials of the party at national and local level. Through his Munich office, Hitler personally controlled the issuing of membership cards for each party member. The party rank and file – who dressed in brown shirts – were expected to take orders from the leader and his selected Nazi elite, without discussion. 'I alone lead the movement', wrote Hitler in 1925, 'and no one can impose conditions on me so long as I personally bear the responsibility' (Shirer, 1961:151). In fact, no local Nazi leader had any legitimacy or authority without the support of the leader. At party conferences, Hitler discouraged delegates from putting forward new policies, and reserved the final decision on all resolutions put to the conference. This simple leadership structure, which had more in common with the army than a political party, had the benefit of being easily understood by all members, and helped keep disparate factions together at crucial points. Anyone who attempted to challenge or criticise Hitler's leadership was very quickly isolated, ostracised and forced to leave the party.

Yet the unique position of the party leader within the organisational structure does not fully explain how the Nazi Party functioned at grassroots level. There was a high degree of disunity and instability within local branches of the Nazi Party. Hitler could not control every member on every issue. He had to devolve power from the centre to regional leaders and local party organisations. This structure led to the creation of a number of regional leaders, and to a number of disputes between them, usually revolving around who was most loyally carrying out the 'Führer's will'. Yet these disputes between regional leaders and party members tended to strengthen Hitler's leadership rather than weaken it, as it allowed him to play one group off against another.

The focal point of Nazi Party organisation was the central office of the party, which was based in Munich (from 1930 it was located at the Brown House). The leader was supported in running the party by his private secretary (Rudolf Hess), who became the second most important party figure, because he opened, and often answered, Hitler's mail, and acted as a key liaison figure between the leader and all other organisational groups within the party at national and local level. Hitler took all the major decisions, but he very often allowed Hess to make some important decisions on his behalf, and most of the routine ones. The other key figures at central office were the chief organisational leader (Gregor Strasser), the executive secretary (Philipp Bouhler), the treasurer (Franz Schwarz), and the propaganda leader (Joseph Goebbels).

In the national organisation of the party, Gregor Strasser, a young radical, originally from Bavaria, was the most powerful figure. As organisational leader, he directed the major activities of the party, and he was also in charge of nine other organisational 'main departments' located at central office, which were led by 'shadow ministers' who formulated policies for the party. This highly centralised organisational structure allowed Strasser to regulate the activities of the party. In July 1932, he headed a total staff at central office numbering 95 people, located in 54 separate offices. On the downside, increasing central control turned the Nazi Party – especially as its popularity and membership expanded – into a top-heavy bureaucracy. More full-time officials – and administrative staff – were employed by the Nazi Party in 1932 than any other German political party. Hitler took pride in the fact that the Nazi Party ensured all party membership forms were

A clean and well-dressed Hitler (pictured at the centre of the back row) in a school photograph during his 4th form in Leonding.

A serious looking Hitler (circled) is pictured with a group of army colleagues during the First World War. The dog in the photo is Foxl, a stray Hitler adopted as his pet.

Hitler speaking at a nationalist meeting at Harzburg in the early 1930s. The man seated next to him (wearing horn-rimmed spectacles) is Alfred Hugenburg, the leader of the DNVP.

Hitler is pictured in front of a group of Stormtroopers at Gera in September 1931, shortly after the Nazi Party had won power in the Thuringia local assembly.

filled out – and signed – at central office, in triplicate, with two copies kept on file, even though this process actually put more strain on the paperwork at central office. The great bulk of Nazi income by the early 1930s was used to pay the salaries of those who worked at central office, and to fund a growing army of paid functionaries at the local level. In practice, central office had to rely on local regional leaders, local party organisations and a large network of ancillary organisations to ensure decisions made at the centre were implemented at the grass roots.

At the local level, the Nazi Party was divided into a large number of regional centres and local branches. Yet at every level of party organisation the leadership principle operated. Each regional leader had authority over those beneath him (they were all male) and took orders from whoever was above him in the party hierarchy. The country was divided for organisational purposes into 34 regional districts (*Gau*), which corresponded roughly with the 34 national electoral districts in the Reichstag. At the centre of all local Nazi Party organisations was the regional leader of the party (the *Gauleiter*), who was not elected by local party activists but was appointed directly by the party leader, and was subject to instant dismissal if he was deemed not to be faithfully carrying out the 'Führer's will'. *Gauleiters* were 'local Führers', who were expected to carry out the 'fundamental directives' issued by the party leader. Although many local *Gauleiters* often pursued their own interests, the majority were loyal to the party leader. Each *Gauleiter* sent a monthly report to central office on a specially printed form which outlined the key activities and developments in his area. Each *Gau* was subdivided into a number of smaller *Kreise* ('circles'), chaired by a *Kreisleiter* (district leader), each of whom was expected to carry out the orders of the *Gauleiter*. These orders were then transmitted further down the chain of command to local branches, which were led by a 'local leader', and then sent on to smaller 'sections', 'cells' and 'tenement blocks'. Anyone joining the Nazi Party in the expectation of engaging in discussions over policy issues would have been very quickly disappointed. The average party activist was expected to be a foot soldier, devoted to the leader, willing to carry out instructions without comment. In order to further encourage party discipline at all levels of the party, central office created 'state inspectors' in 1932, who had the power to investigate local party organisations. In addition, there was also an Investigation and Mediation Committee (USCHLA), which operated as a national tribunal to arbitrate over any disputes at the local level, and had the power to expel individuals and close down local party organisations (Fischer, 1995).

The Nazi Party also created a host of ancillary organisations, including National Socialist leagues of teachers, doctors, students, civil servants, farmers, youth and women. The most important ancillary organisations of the party before 1933 were the SA, the Hitler Youth, the National Socialist

Factory Cell Organisation and the Agricultural Affairs Bureau. As we saw in Chapter 3, the SA, led by Ernst Roehm, consisted of ex-soldiers who not only protected Nazi meetings but also provided a strong army of committed – and very violent – activists to put out on the streets in direct competition against the communists. The SA had been the heart of the pre-1923 party, but it was banned by the German government in the aftermath of the failed Munich putsch. It was more firmly established in urban areas, and its members tended to come from the more 'socialist' and 'anti-capitalist' wing of the party. It was only in the late 1920s that the SA was allowed to operate again, and then only on the condition it remained a purely non-military body. The leaders of the SA remained sceptical about the 'parliamentary' and 'legal' route to power, and remained wedded to the idea of overthrowing Weimar democracy by force. The rank and file of the SA accepted their role as the 'foot soldiers' of the movement with great reluctance, primarily because they were dependent on financial support from the party. The members of the SA had a romantic allegiance to Hitler as leader, but they were never completely under the control of central office. The SA viewed the concentration on winning elections – especially after 1930 – as a sign its own position within the party as a street-fighting force was being downgraded and marginalised. Between 1929 and 1933, the membership of the SA grew from 30,000 to 425,000. Most members were males between the ages of 18 and 35. The SA offered an outlet for many delinquent young men to channel their anti-social and violent proclivities against political opponents, particularly in the major cities. The SA hardly ever attacked the police during demonstrations, and they generally goaded their left-wing opponents to start a fight by parading in a highly provocative manner through areas where their political opponents lived. Hitler wanted the SA to 'conquer the streets' by out-shouting and generally making life difficult for their most hated political opponents, the communists. It was often extremely difficult to restrain the hot-blooded and violent elements in the SA, who doubted whether the 'parliamentary' road to power was the right one to travel along. One demand the SA sought (but which Hitler opposed) was for their members to be afforded dominance in military matters over the regular army, should the Nazis gain power. Hitler never really moulded the SA into the obedient 'political' army he wanted it to be. Indeed, the blood purge of the SA ordered by Hitler in the summer of 1934, under pressure from the army, was not entirely unpredictable, given the troubled relationship that existed between the SA and the political leadership of the party before 1933.

The Nazi Party was very successful in attracting young people, and created its own organisations for them: the Hitler Youth (*Hitler-Jugend*), which indoctrinated young members of the party with Nazi ideas on leadership, race, discipline and military values. The Nazi Party offered the young a seemingly brighter future, which appears to have attracted many of them to support the party. By the summer of 1932, the Hitler Youth boasted 100,000 members, with most of these recruits coming from younger members of the middle classes. Indeed, the Hitler Youth started to incorporate the members of traditional middle-class and lower middle-class youth groups into its organisation as Nazi popularity increased. It sent young people to summer camps at which physical fitness, rifle practice, and team-building games were high on the agenda. The German Girls' League, an equivalent female organisation, encouraged young girls to improve their fitness, but mostly concentrated on developing the domestic skills required of a future wife and mother. The Hitler Youth mobilised large numbers of young people, and created a close camaraderie among its members. Members of the Hitler Youth before 1933 later recalled that 'no social or class distinctions' operated within the organisation (Allen, 1995: 73).

The Agricultural Affairs Bureau, another important Nazi ancillary organisation, led by Richard Darré, helped to persuade farmers and agricultural workers to support the Nazi Party. It provided expert commentary, specialist speakers on agricultural matters, and established a newspaper (*National-Sozialistische Landpost*) with a wide circulation in farming regions. The Nazi Party promised to introduce significant land reform to help drag farmers out of the 'great depression'. The specialised work of the Agricultural Affairs Bureau constantly highlighted the sorry plight of farmers. It appears this strategy did pay dividends, as the growth in Nazi electoral support from 1930 onwards was higher in rural areas, especially in places where the Agricultural Affairs Bureau had been most active.

The party also attempted, though with much less success, to gain support from members of the industrial working class by creating the National Socialist Factory Cell Organisation (NSBO) during the early 1930s. The idea of setting up grass-roots supporters of Nazism among factory workers emanated from the more 'socialist' wing of the party, predominantly based in the northern regions of Germany. In the spring of 1931, Gregor Strasser launched the 'Into the Factories' campaign, which aimed to increase working-class support for the Nazi Party in industrial areas. Towards the end of 1932, 250,000 workers were members of the NSBO. Yet Hitler refused to support the establishment of Nazi trade union organisations, which tended to weaken greatly the appeal of the NSBO among factory workers. Indeed, when the Nazis came to power, most trade union rights were removed, and the NSBO, because it ignored the wishes of the employer and favoured those of the employee, was deemed incompatible with National Socialist ideology and forced to disband. It was replaced under Nazi rule by the Labour Front (the DAF) led by Robert Ley, which aimed to create 'a social and productive community' which defined the employer as 'master' and the employee as 'follower'.

There is little doubt that the Nazi Party, although not free of factional rivalries and disagreements, did possess a very efficient centralised organisational apparatus. It also possessed a leader whose speaking powers were a match for any other party. There were also many figures within the party, most notably Goebbels and Strasser, who had great propaganda and organisational skills, which were also the envy of other parties. In addition, the party had many committed and self-sacrificing local leaders and activists, a strong group of paramilitary supporters in the SA willing to engage in violence with political opponents, and a growing youth movement.

PROPAGANDA

A second key factor which greatly contributed to the rise to power of the Nazi Party was effective propaganda. In *Mein Kampf*, Hitler devoted two chapters to this subject. According to Hitler, the mass of the people, of whom he had a very low opinion, could be easily influenced by means of the constant repetition of a number of key slogans and images of effective propaganda. Nazi propaganda was centrally controlled and organised by Dr Joseph Goebbels (the original spin doctor), who was appointed head of party propaganda in November 1928. It is no coincidence that the great surge in Nazi electoral support took place in the period after Goebbels took control of Nazi Party propaganda.

At the heart of Nazi propaganda was the spoken word, delivered in its most powerful form by Adolf Hitler, whose speeches, using microphones and loudspeakers, became a major focal point of the appeal of the Nazi Party to electors. At party rallies and public meetings, Hitler's entrance was always delayed – to build up the tension slowly. When he appeared, he was accompanied by a torchlight procession of flag-bearing and drum-beating supporters, while music played and searchlights flashed all around the arena. Hitler presented himself in his speeches as a humble soldier whose life work was to restore the honour of Germany. The Nuremberg rally, held annually from 1927 onwards, was a quasi-religious event: organised with great theatrical flair, it gave a powerful display of Nazi passion [*Doc. 15*].

Yet stage-managed rallies at which Hitler appeared were only one, albeit important, aspect of Nazi propaganda activity. The Nazi message was relayed by a large number of party-appointed public speakers at meetings held throughout the country. Some of the other leading Nazis, particularly Goebbels, gained a high reputation as orators, but it was a large band of specialist speakers that carried the Nazi message into local areas. All speakers were required to undertake training, and they needed authorisation from central office before they were allowed to operate. Registered Nazi-approved speakers were required, even when qualified, to submit the text of their speeches to national party headquarters for final approval. The

Nazis often employed former army officers, U-boat captains, farmers, teachers and even some pastors to give speeches. Joseph Goebbels kept local branches supplied with up-to-date information on key electoral issues and often gave instructions as to how local party workers were to present issues to potential voters [*Doc. 19*]. One of the greatest strengths of Nazi propaganda was the way local speakers were allowed to tailor their message to reflect policies and fears and prejudices in different areas of the country. Another innovative aspect of Nazi propaganda activity at the local level was the holding of meetings not only before and during elections, but also in the time between them. This active form of campaigning meant the Nazi Party – unlike its leading political opponents – was always attempting to reinforce solidarity among existing supporters and to attract new converts.

The Nazi Party also created a key visual propaganda symbol in the Nazi flag, which proved extremely effective. The flag, with its distinctive and visually memorable Swastika logo – designed by Hitler – was a potent symbol of party identity. It was basically red (borrowing that colour from the popular communist red flag) but in its centre was a white circle, to represent the pure Aryan heritage, with the visually memorable black Swastika symbol, borrowed from earlier *Volkisch* sects, in the centre. The flag ingeniously incorporated the red of socialism with the traditional black and white of the pre-1914 imperial flag.

Goebbels created many memorable posters, which included such key Nazi slogans as 'Hitler – Germany's last chance', 'One People, One Nation, One Leader' ('ein Volk, ein Reich, ein Führer'), and 'Germany Awake'. Nazi posters always depicted workers in favourable terms, but portrayed communists, usually as bearded 'foreigners', with definite Semitic looks, manipulating the workers for their own ends. Most democratic politicians, especially those associated with the 'betrayal' of Germany during the First World War, were shown as fat hypocrites, dining on champagne and caviar. Most Nazi electoral posters were anti-Marxist and anti-communist, while most anti-Semitic posters were confined to Nazi newspapers. In many rural areas, Nazi propaganda had a free run as neither the Communist Party, which had few supporters in such areas, nor the traditional democratic parties bothered to use propaganda heavily in these areas.

The Nazi Party also used the press – with much less success – to spread its gospel to potential followers. Hitler believed the press was of great importance in helping to mould public opinion. To this end, the Nazis set up a number of 'in house' newspapers, including a national daily newspaper, the *Völkischer Beobachter*, and many other local newspapers, most notably *The Attack (Der Angriff)* based in Berlin. However, the sales of Nazi newspapers were poor. In September 1930, for example, the *Völkischer Beobachter* sold only 100,000 copies. Nazi newspapers were quite good at creating blood-curdling headlines, and they often used photographs effectively, but the general quality of the journalism was poor. Nazi newspapers concentrated on a very small number of themes, and the articles in them were written in a very uninspiring and repetitive manner. After 1930, the Nazis benefited from receiving very favourable coverage in many of the leading regional papers controlled by Alfred Hugenberg, the leader of the conservative National People's Party (DNVP).

The Nazis in power are always associated with the effective use of film in propaganda, in which they are often seen – especially in modern TV documentaries – to be ahead of their time. Before 1933, however, even though it established the National Socialist Film Service in 1928, the party did not make extensive use of film in its propaganda activities. They did show some propaganda films, using party-owned projectors and screens, in some remote rural areas during election campaigns. We also know that the newsreel company Ufa, owned by Hugenberg, allowed the Nazis a platform in many of the newsreels shown in cinemas throughout Germany during the early 1930s. However, the actual number of times Adolf Hitler appeared in newsreels was limited, and film cannot be viewed as a major aspect of Nazi propaganda before 1933. In fact, many of the existing German democratic parties, most notably the liberal DDP and the DNVP, made much greater use of film than did the Nazi Party.

It is important to examine some of the key themes of Nazi Party propaganda. In attacking their opponents, the Nazis were great exponents of what is now called 'negative campaigning'. They blamed the economic depression and high unemployment on the failings of the Weimar democratic system. The 'Marxists' (and to a lesser extent 'Jews') were depicted in Nazi propaganda as the key enemies of the German people. Alongside this 'negative campaigning', the Nazis emphasised the positive aspects of their own 'movement'. Above all, Nazi propaganda projected Hitler as the charismatic saviour of the German people. Indeed, such was the dominance of Hitler in the projection of the Nazi Party, it became commonplace for most German newspapers, and most political opponents, to describe the party in articles and speeches as 'the Hitler movement'.

A great many historians would suggest Nazi propaganda appealed most persuasively to the middle classes. There was a distinct change in the focus of Nazi propaganda after 1928, away from attempting to appeal to the 'workers' in urban centres, and towards targeting middle-class voters, especially those in rural areas with no strong pre-existing political allegiances [*Doc. 14*]. The Nazis also tried to win over the working classes, and kept on stressing the broad 'national' appeal of their programme, but it became increasingly apparent to Nazi activists that their appeals to patriotism, a strong leader, anti-Marxism, and the creation of a folk community were being received far more sympathetically in middle-class areas of the cities, and in rural areas.

MEMBERSHIP

The social profile of members of the Nazi Party has been the subject of detailed scrutiny among historians. The prevalent view in this debate suggests the Nazi Party was dominated by the middle classes, or more specifically the lower middle class (Kater, 1983). In more recent times, however, this view has been challenged by a counter-argument which suggests the Nazi Party was a genuine 'people's party' whose membership was drawn from all social groups in German society, with a substantial working-class element (Muhlberger, 1991).

The Nazi Party began life, as we have already seen, as an anti-parliamentary and revolutionary antidote to the growing appeal of socialism among the working classes. It was envisaged at the outset as an alternative to existing socialist parties which appealed to the working classes, such as the SPD and the Communist Party (KPD). Yet the Nazi Party never attracted a sizeable number of members as converts from either of these parties. Very few active communists, socialists, trade unionists or factory workers, located in the major urban centres, ever joined the Nazi Party. On the contrary, these people proved the most hostile to the party and relatively immune from its appeal.

The membership of the early Nazi Party, located in Munich from 1919 to 1923, was dominated by males from middle-class and lower middle-class groups, most notably skilled independent craftsmen, small businessmen, merchants, office workers, low-ranking civil servants, teachers and farmers. Very few women ever became official party members, nor were they encouraged to join. By and large, the early members of the Nazi Party consisted of people – even those within the middle class – who were anti-parliamentary, and most often politically adrift from the mainstream democratic political parties. It is also noticeable in the early membership lists of the party how many 'renegade' members of the upper middle class, the former aristocracy and university students keep appearing. Most of these members viewed the Nazi Party as a potential counter-revolutionary movement which could restore their pre-1914 position within German society by destroying democracy. These upper- middle and middle-class supporters were more likely to be old-style conservatives, and the natural supporters of right-wing nationalist and conservative parties. Much less prominent on the membership lists of the party in its early days are industrial 'unskilled workers'. Indeed, this group, even though the party called itself a 'Workers' Party', formed a minority among the membership even during the early years in Munich. The Nazi Party was much more successful in attracting the disgruntled skilled worker, or the self-employed independent artisan, because these workers viewed themselves as a cut above the level of the 'proletarian' worker, and the prejudices against Jews, which the Nazis emphasised, were already prominent in these groups but were much less pronounced among the working classes. As one historian puts it, 'fascism was the socialism of the petit-bourgeoisie' (Fischer, 1995: 91).

In the period from 1924 to 1929, when the Nazi Party became more nationally based, there was a sharp increase in membership. The greatest proportion of new members in this period came from the Protestant middle class, the petit bourgeois lower-middle-class and small landholding groups. More small businessmen and independent skilled workers joined the party between 1924 and 1929. Among this group, it was the owners of small and medium-sized firms and wholesalers rather than those who owned large factories who became members.

After 1928, largely due to its successful propaganda efforts, the Nazi Party started to attract increasing numbers of members among small farmers. It seems many of these people had not owed allegiance to any other political party before they joined the Nazis and they were attracted by the Nazi idea of a folk community, in which agricultural self-sufficiency would be a central aim. Farmers – and agricultural workers – started to view the party as a potential saviour of the agricultural sector. It was also in the period from 1928 onwards that the party started to attract growing numbers of the new white-collar workers, lower-grade civil servants and middle-class professionals. The Nazi Party also continued to attract teachers, even though they were subject to possible disciplinary action – even dismissal – for joining the party. The membership lists after 1928 contain larger numbers of the upper middle classes. In 1930, 50 per cent of all German university students were members of the Nazi Party, which seems a surprisingly high figure considering that it was a very anti-intellectual party which showed contempt for 'book learned academics'.

The Nazi Party continued to make energetic efforts to attract new working-class members in heavily industrialised areas, but such workers remained relatively immune to these initiatives. By and large, the industrial working class were not attracted, except in very small and isolated pockets, to join the Nazi Party. Those 'workers' who did join tended to come from small towns and villages without a strong tradition of socialism. The Nazi 'working class' member tended to resemble 'working-class conservatives' in Britain, and identified with the middle classes. Overall, the Nazi Party, although it did attract more 'workers' in the period 1924–30, continued to be a predominantly lower middle-class party, which was becoming increasingly attractive to the upper class, to small businessmen, white-collar workers and people who lived in small towns and villages without any strong political allegiance to any of the traditional parties.

It was in the period from 1930 to 1933 that Nazi Party membership – and electoral support – increased sharply. It was also during this period that the party, though it still insisted it spoke for 'all national groups', began to direct its propaganda towards the traditional concerns of middle-class Germans, and attempted to attract rural members in greater numbers. In this period, the backbone of the Nazi Party continued to be members from this group tended to be lower than it had been from 1924 to 1930. The group which greatly increased its membership of the party came from the upper middle class and the former aristocracy. Many of these new members were from 'old' conservative middle-class groups already hostile to the Weimar Republic, who started to view the Nazi Party as a viable alternative to the traditional right-wing DNVP. It is also noticeable after 1929 how Hitler began to downgrade the 'socialist' aspects of the Nazi programme in favour of its nationalistic elements. There was a definite increase in support from small businessmen and even from some major industrialists such as Fritz Thyssen, Hugo Stinnes and Albert Vogler after 1930, though this group remained under-represented in the party as a whole. Many large landowning farmers started to join the party. They appear to have been attracted by the Nazi promise to give the revival of agriculture a top priority within the new national community. The party was also successful in attracting growing numbers of upper middle-class professionals and high-ranking civil servants as members from 1930 onwards. There is little doubt that something very significant was happening among some sections of the Protestant German middle classes during the period after 1930: most of them were coming increasingly to believe that the Nazi Party, with its promise to give aid to farmers and protection to business from foreign competition, could drag Germany out of political and economic crisis [*Doc. 17*]. Yet the Nazis did not appeal to all members of the middle classes. The Catholic parts of Germany, which accounted for a third of the population, were not receptive to the Nazi Party and remained loyal to the Catholic Centre Party. Hence, if Nazism was a middle-class revolt, it was a Protestant one.

The Nazi Party also attracted its largest influx of 'workers' between 1930 and 1933. It gained more converts from former supporters of the SPD in industrial areas than it had ever done before. At the same time, the polarisation between Nazis and communists became much stronger than ever before, with their street battles in big cities becoming a serious law-and-order problem.

From 1930 to 1933, the Nazi Party attracted a broader spectrum of support than at any time in its history. It is also true that in 1932 approximately 40 per cent of party members came from working-class backgrounds. There were certainly more working-class members joining the party after 1930 than in any other period. However, when attention is focused more closely on these new 'working-class' members of the party, it can be seen that most were craft workers, agricultural labourers, and those workers employed in small companies, without a strong trade union presence. The party still encountered difficulties, even at the height of its pre-1933 electoral popularity, in attracting factory workers who were also members of trade unions in the major urban industrial centres. It was workers who felt themselves above the level of the 'proletariat', and those who were antagonistic towards socialism, who joined the party. These 'working-class Nazis' possessed upwardly mobile aspirations. It seems most of these 'workers' shifted their support from the non-socialist parties, and from right-wing 'nationalist' fringe groups rather than from either the communists or the Social Democrats, although the Nazis did gain some converts from these groups. It is often thought the Nazi Party attracted more support from the urban unemployed during the early 1930s than the Nazis. Indeed, the Nazis gained more support from white-collar workers, civil servants and professionals who were still in work but feared they might become unemployed. In rural areas, the Nazis were able to mobilise 'workers' who seemingly had no previous political allegiance to any political party. Most urban industrialised and unionised workers did not join the Nazi Party. In rural Protestant communities, especially in the north, large numbers of agricultural labourers joined the party. Again, this group had very little affinity with socialism, nor any strong pre-existing allegiance to trade unions. New recruits in rural areas seem to have been attracted by the idea, put forward in Nazi propaganda, that a Nazi government would bring about a 'new deal' for rural Germany [*Doc. 14*]. Most new recruits to the Nazi party (48.6 per cent) from 1930 onwards came from the middle class. At the same time, the upper middle class were joining the party in far higher numbers than ever before. Many of the existing working-class members – especially those in the SA – were very alarmed about the increasingly 'bourgeois' direction in which the party was moving after 1930.

It must be accepted that the lower middle class and middle class were always over-represented among the membership of the Nazi Party. Indeed, party membership records suggest that it was predominantly a lower-middle-class party which extended its solid core from 1930 onwards to incorporate greater numbers of the upper middle classes, and attracted many new working-class supporters and 'workers' in rural areas. However, it must also be emphasised that the Nazi Party attracted a broader cross-section of members than any other Weimar political party. This can be ascribed in a very great measure to Hitler's clever ploy of portraying the party as a respectable 'nationalist' and 'conservative' party willing to work within the existing system, while downplaying its previous ambiguous relationship with 'socialism' and its former commitment to the violent overthrow of the state.

CHAPTER SIX

HITLER'S RISE TO POWER

At the end of 1924, the future of the Nazi Party seemed in serious doubt. Adolf Hitler, the most well-known figure in the party, was in jail for high treason, and the party and the SA were both banned and had split apart into rival factions. While serving his sentence in the Landsberg fortress, Hitler became convinced the Nazi Party could only win power by legal means through electoral success, and enact a 'legal revolution' to build a dictatorship afterwards [Doc. 7]. This was likely to prove a long-drawn-out process, for three reasons. First, the right-wing movement had broken into a large number of small factions, without any clear direction or leadership. Second, the severe crisis in the Germany economy (dubbed the 'great inflation') had come to an end, and the period following was one of relative economic prosperity. Third, the army had lost interest in overthrowing the state or collaborating with right-wing extra-parliamentary groups (Orlow, 1969).

REBUILDING THE NAZI PARTY

While Hitler was incarcerated, the Nazi Party had split into two different groups: the Greater German People's Party, which included the nucleus of the Munich branch of the party, and the National Socialist Freedom Party, composed of the more 'socialist' elements in northern Germany. The only saving grace as far as Hitler was concerned was that both groups pledged their support for him. In December 1924, when he was released on parole, he was almost back to where he had started in 1919. Neither of the Nazi splinter groups had made any real impact in his absence. At a party meeting on 27 February 1925, Hitler announced he would pursue a 'legal path to power', promising to work within the constitution. Even this would be difficult as the Nazi leader was banned from making public speeches in Bavaria, and from speaking in many other German states.

Hitler realised he would have to reinvent the Nazi Party, from a rabble-rousing, street-fighting force into a national party with a national organisation. This did not mean the Nazi Party was to become democratic in outlook or organisation. In fact, one of Hitler's first acts on leaving prison was to tell his supporters he wanted to remain an unconditional and all-powerful leader of the party. He also decided to retain Munich as the centre of all party activities. The rank and file in the Bavarian capital accepted Hitler back as the undisputed 'Führer' of the party without much dissent. Outside Munich, the Nazi leader had more trouble reasserting his authority. The northern wing of the party had always been more 'socialist' and 'anti-capitalist' in outlook than the ultra-nationalist and pro-army Munich wing. Most of the northern 'socialists' believed Hitler was, at heart, a 'soldier radical', whose real sympathies were with the younger 'progressive' socialist wing of the party, rather than with the anti-republican forces in the Bavarian wing of the party who were closely aligned with renegade members of the upper classes and the army. The strongest supporters of the view that the newly formulated Nazi Party needed to become more 'radical' and 'socialist' if it was to achieve electoral success were Gregor Strasser, its organisational leader, Otto Strasser, his brother, and Joseph Goebbels, who was in charge of propaganda. The northern group wanted the reborn Nazi Party to compete for votes in the large urban and industrial areas of Germany [*Doc. 8*]. In these areas, their opponents would be the working-class socialist parties, the SPD and the KPD – parties that appealed to workers who were members of trade unions and were anti-capitalist in outlook.

Adolf Hitler, who tried to keep his own views quiet, and most of the Munich wing of the party were not keen on the idea of moving the party in a definite 'socialist' direction in search of votes. Hitler believed such a move would alienate potential middle-class support and antagonise the conservative groups with whom he thought he needed to collaborate in order to come to power. Accordingly, Hitler opposed the creation of Nazi trade unions, while skilfully keeping his own rather pro-capitalist and anti-socialist views to himself.

Yet the 'Strasser' wing of the party continued to urge Hitler to adopt the 'socialist' strategy they favoured after his release from prison. To stress their socialist credentials, the northern group came out in favour of the controversial policy of confiscating the land of the former Hohenzollern princes, and then redistributing it to local peasants, if they gained power. This stance was a clear break with the pre-1914 'old guard', and Hitler was opposed to it, because he did not want to alienate what he saw as a group very favourable to the militaristic nationalism he most passionately favoured.

To resolve this dispute, Hitler called a party meeting, which included members of both the northern and southern wings of the party, at Bamberg on 4 February 1926. Bamberg was very close to Munich, which made it easier for Hitler to pack the meeting with his loyal – non-'socialist' – colleagues. The real issue at stake at the Bamberg meeting was whether the Nazi Party would remain a 'Führer' party, in which the leader's authority was paramount, or whether authority was to be derived from the party programme, which could be altered by pressure from factions within the various regional sections of the party. At the meeting, Hitler gained acceptance for the principle that he was the undisputed leader of the Nazi Party. He also asked all members to pledge support for the existing 1920 programme of the party, which was regarded as 'unalterable' and did contain some commitment to so-called socialist principles. As the 'expropriation' of monarchical land had never been included in the original programme, Hitler persuaded the northern wing to drop their support for this policy as a means of expressing public unity within the party. Before the Bamberg meeting, Hitler had used his personal charm to win over Joseph Goebbels to his side, which greatly helped him to increase his authority in the northern wing of the party. By the end of 1926, therefore, Hitler had re-established his disciplined control over the party and its policies.

At the time, Hitler's triumph over the 'socialist' wing of the party at Bamberg was a hollow one, as all the Nazi leader had gained was the right to lead a very small and insignificant political party, which seemed to have little prospect of becoming a major force in German politics. For a party that thrived on despair, the political conditions in the post-1924 period were worryingly optimistic. The outward signs of economic recovery were all around. Unemployment fell, wages increased, inflation came under control, and there was a general feel-good factor, no matter how illusory it proved to be. Even to the rest of the world, Germany appeared reborn. In 1926, the German government joined the League of Nations, accepted the western territorial arrangements of the Paris peace settlement (under the Locarno treaties), and was even making regular reparations payments with the help of US loans. In this stable political and economic climate, the appeal of the Nazi Party, and other extreme right-wing parties, retreated to the periphery.

THE ECLIPSE OF SOCIALISM IN THE NAZI PARTY

The decision of the Nazi Party to choose the very slow 'legal path' to power meant it had to distance itself from various paramilitary groups which had previously supported it. There was also a pressing need for the party to decide how it was going to appeal to voters. Focusing exclusively on Hitler's charismatic speaking abilities was not an option, in the short term at least, because of the speaking ban on the Nazi leader, which remained in force until September 1928.

After some discussion, the 'socialist' north German elements in the party, whose power and influence was increasing at this time, persuaded a somewhat sceptical Hitler to adopt the 'Urban Plan' in 1926. This strategy concentrated on building up electoral support for the Nazi Party in major industrial cities, in direct competition with the two major working-class parties in these areas, the KPD and the SPD. From 1926 onwards, therefore, the Nazi Party adopted a strong, 'anti-capitalist' tone, and persistently attacked the 'decadence' of the upper middle classes for continuing to support the Weimar Republic. Although Hitler doubted whether the party should concentrate its electoral strategy on attracting working-class voters in urban areas at the expense of alienating potential support among the middle-class groups and the hard core of lower middle-class support for the party in the south, he went along with the Urban Plan.

Not surprisingly, the much trumpeted Urban Plan was a complete failure. Most industrial workers in the major cities remained loyal to the KPD and the SPD, and continued to view the Nazis as a reactionary, right-wing party opposed to socialism, and not genuinely anti-capitalist or pro-socialist. At the beginning of 1928, Hitler, who was always sceptical about the likely success of winning over the working classes to National Socialism in the first place, was able to downgrade, then abandon, the Urban Plan. Henceforth, the Nazi Party, although it did not completely abandon attempting to win working-class electoral support, placed much greater emphasis on a new dual electoral strategy, which involved attracting greater middle-class support and winning over – for the first time – disaffected rural voters.

ECONOMIC COLLAPSE IN GERMANY

Less than a year after the Nazi Party decided to take its message to middle-class and rural voters, economic gloom returned. The economic recovery of the mid-1920s, which had established political stability, was based on the very shaky foundation of US loans, which stopped after the collapse of the Wall Street stock market in October 1929. Unemployment now spread like a plague throughout Germany, growing from 1.4 million to 6 million of the insured population, and affecting millions of families between 1928 and 1932. In the same period, there was a flight of capital from Germany, a 42 per cent fall in industrial production and a devastating collapse in agricultural prices. Everyone in Germany was affected in some way by the depression. At first, the economic downturn hit bankers and businessmen, but, as it deepened, farmers, small shopkeepers, agricultural labourers, workers in light industry, pensioners, white-collar workers and even members of the middle-class professions all suffered. The political effects for the Weimar Republic were equally catastrophic. The fragile centre coalition led by Hermann Müller, which included members of the SDP, the liberal DVP (the German People's Party) and the Catholic Centre Party, fell from power in March 1930. From this point onwards, Germany was a veiled dictatorship, with each Chancellor ruling, with the consent of President Hindenberg, under emergency powers granted under Article 48 of the fragile Weimar constitution.

THE EMERGENCE OF HITLER ON THE NATIONAL STAGE

It was during the period of the 'Great Depression' that electoral support for the Nazi Party grew remarkably. A very interesting 'if' question would be to consider what would have happened to Germany had there been no economic depression. It is possible that Hitler might never have come to power. But whether Germany would have remained a democracy, and lived at peace with the rest of Europe during the 1930s and 1940s, seems equally unlikely. There was an underlying anti-democratic mood in Germany which economic depression magnified, but did not create. The anti-democratic mood in Germany was like the wind: you could not see it, but when it went past it made trees bend [*Doc. 13*].

After 1929, that wind was blowing at gale force. It would, however, be unfair, as some historians have suggested, to assert that any right-wing, anti-democratic party could have prospered in these gloomy economic circumstances. This is to underestimate completely how skilfully Hitler exploited the effects of economic depression to win electoral support for the Nazi Party. It also downplays the importance of the decision taken by the Nazis before the economic collapse to concentrate on winning over greater middle-class support and attracting voters in the rural areas. In fact, Adolf Hitler had waited very patiently, and had predicted bad times were just around the corner. Once they arrived, he grasped his opportunity to exploit them with quite exceptional ability: he offered certain sections of German society the hope of deliverance from the misery all around them; he offered a faith in the German people and optimism for the future of Germany under Nazi rule which none of his political rivals could remotely match; and he opposed everything, and promised everything, but with a passion and vision which many Germans found incredibly seductive [*Doc. 17*]. Unlike the other parties in the German system, which represented very specific and often narrow interest groups, Hitler emphasised the 'national' appeal of the Nazi Party. This allowed the party to win votes from those who had previously supported narrow, small special interest parties, especially those operating in rural areas and small towns.

It must also be emphasised that Hitler was already emerging on the national political stage before the Wall Street crash occurred. In the summer of 1929, he joined forces with a number of right-wing groups, including the Pan-Germans, the Agrarian League and the German National People's

Party (DNVP) led by Alfred Hugenberg, a middle-class and traditional conservative, in opposition to the Young Plan, which outlined a reduced scale of reparations payments for the German government by extending the payments until 1988. With the help of Hugenberg's newsreel company, his newspaper interests and close business allies, the Nazi leader used the referendum on the Young Plan to mount his first major national speaking tour since the early days of the Nazi Party. Although the campaign ended in failure, the support Hitler received from many traditional right-wing groups during it gave him greater national publicity and respectability than he had ever received before. Hitler was being talked of, after 1929, in some sections of the 'respectable' right-wing parts of the German press as a possible leader and unifier of the diffuse and seemingly moribund German right. During the campaign against the Young Plan, Hitler's dynamic oratory was shown to be a key political weapon for the Nazi Party, and it was suggested that the more he was exposed to the wider public the greater would his popularity – and that of the party – increase.

In spite of the useful alliance Hitler had brokered with the traditional right during the campaign against the Young Plan, many on the left of the Nazi Party still continued to press for a more definite socialist commitment from the party leader. The divisions within the party came into public view in a debate in 1930 between Hitler and Otto Strasser, a leading figure in the 'anti-capitalist' grouping within the party. Otto Strasser suggested the Nazi Party was gradually turning – with Hitler's support – into a respectable, pro-capitalist, anti-Marxist, middle-class party, which increasingly depicted the working class as the enemy. In response, Hitler claimed 'socialism' – as far as he was concerned – meant something very different from the anti-capitalist version being peddled by Strasser. 'I have never said that all enterprises should be socialised', claimed Hitler. 'On the contrary, I have maintained that we might socialise enterprises prejudicial to the interests of the state.' At the end of this heated exchange, Strasser remained dissatisfied with Hitler's pro-capitalist version of socialism, which hardly differed from the reactionary version of the traditional conservative right [*Doc. 11*].

Overall, the Hitler–Strasser debate helped the Nazi leader to win greater middle-class support for the party, as he suggested National Socialism was not really a type of socialism which threatened the power of the capitalist owners of industry. On the contrary, Hitler had raised the attractive prospect of forging an alliance with the traditional right in order to destroy the power of socialism and 'Jews' in Germany.

THE NAZI ELECTORAL BREAKTHROUGH

The German national elections in September 1930 provided Hitler with an ideal opportunity to play on the anxiety of middle-class and rural German voters in the midst of the 'Great Depression'. The Nazi Party showed a remarkable surge of voter support in the contest, increasing its seats in the Reichstag from 12 to 107, and its share of the overall vote from 810,000 in 1928 to 6.4 million (representing 18 per cent of total votes), to become the second largest political party in Germany. In one election, the Nazi Party had advanced from insignificance to national prominence. No comparable breakthrough can be found in the entire history of German politics. Of the existing middle-class 'bourgeois' parties, only the Catholic Centre Party maintained its electoral position. The conservative DNVP, the party which had allied with Hitler during the campaign against the Young Plan, saw its share of the votes fall from 14.3 per cent to 7 per cent. The SPD suffered a severe fall in electoral support, but the communist KPD actually increased its vote from 10.6 per cent to 13 per cent of the overall vote.

NAZI ELECTORAL SUPPORT

The sudden surge of electoral support for the Nazi Party from 1930 onwards requires some explanation. Obviously, the economic depression had some impact. Many voters were registering a 'bitterness' or 'protest' vote in the middle of a severe economic downturn. However, this explanation provides only part of the answer. A great deal of credit must also be given to Adolf Hitler, and the efficient Nazi Party propaganda machine, for persuading voters to see the Nazis as the major outlet for their frustration with the economic circumstances, and the apparent inability of the Weimar system to cope with them. Nazi Party rallies during the election campaign were much better stage-managed than those of any other party. At these rallies, the feeling of being involved in something much greater than a mere political meeting was very powerful. Many 'floating voters' who attended these rallies later recalled they felt they were being caught up in something resembling the emergence of a great passionate religious movement rather than attending a traditional democratic party meeting [*Doc. 15*]. The Nazis were also successful in gaining a foothold among important middle-class occupational groups, including teachers, engineers and lawyers. The party was extremely popular among university students, while the Hitler Youth offered young people responsibility, and helped to provide the party with many future party activists and voters.

Above all, Hitler had transformed himself from an impulsive street fighter with the gift of the gab into a shrewd and flexible politician with tremendous oratorical skills. His decision to pursue the 'legal path to power' ensured the rebuilt Nazi Party became a centrally coordinated national party, with a successful propaganda machine, which mobilised voters in many areas that had shown little prior interest in politics. The decision to move the party in a more middle-class and rural direction after 1928 – which Hitler supported – enabled the party to become more 'respectable', and to tap into the discontent these groups felt during the depression.

Electoral statistics show the Nazi Party drew support from all classes, but not from all religious groups. Nazi voting strength was much higher in the Protestant rural areas of the north German plain, stretching from east Prussia to Schleswig-Holstein, than anywhere else. The Nazis could not weaken support for the Catholic Centre Party. The religious factor is very evident in the election results in Bavaria. Most of the Protestants lived in the north of the region, and in these districts the Nazis did very well. In southern Bavaria, however, which was overwhelmingly Catholic, the Nazi vote was amongst the lowest anywhere in Germany.

By and large, the major electoral gains for the Nazi Party from 1930 onwards came at the expense of the large number of right-wing special interest parties, and by an influx from former supporters of the DNVP. The Nazis were always able to win votes more easily from people who had previously supported very small parties, and in regions where they faced no major competition from traditional parties.

It must be emphasised that, with few exceptions, the Nazis were much more popular with voters in small towns than in the large urban cities and industrial regions. In the major cities, the Nazi vote was at its weakest. The only areas of big cities where the Nazis did well tended to be in upper middle-class, suburban, affluent residential areas, whose traditional allegiance had previously been to right-wing conservative parties. In the July 1932 national election, for example, in German cities with a population exceeding 100,000 Nazi electoral support was 10 per cent lower than in small towns. Working-class Nazi voters usually came from towns with a population of less than 5000. The hard core of Nazi electoral support in the September 1930 election came from the lower middle class in rural Protestant areas such as small shopkeepers, independent skilled workers, tradesmen, farmers and agricultural labourers. At the July 1932 election, the Nazis gained electoral support from white-collar workers and upper middle-class Protestants in affluent suburbs in large cities as well as from professionals such as teachers, doctors, civil servants and engineers.

The major proportion of Nazi working-class support came from rural workers and labourers, and from workers in small-scale craft and domestic industries who were hostile towards trade unions and communism. The Nazi Party failed to win substantial support from members of trade unions, and from the majority of industrial workers in the big cities, the bulk of whom remained loyal to the KPD and to the SPD. More surprising is the failure of the party to gain support from the ranks of the unemployed, even though this group, featured heavily in Nazi propaganda posters. In areas with the highest concentrations of unemployed industrial workers, the KPD did best, enjoying over 60 per cent of the vote.

Even so, it would be wrong to depict the Nazi Party merely as a Protestant, rural, predominantly middle-class phenomenon, even though it cannot be denied that such voters were its primary supporters. What the Nazi Party achieved was to gain votes from a much broader cross-section of the German electorate than any other German political party.

The growth in electoral support for the Nazi Party from 1930 to 1933 was a vital factor in Hitler's rise to power because it placed the Nazi leader in a position to lead a right-wing authoritarian government, with popular appeal, if that option became favoured by President Hindenburg. It was, therefore, the German people who voted for Hitler in democratic elections who placed him in a central political position from where he was able to place pressure on Hindenburg and his political advisers to invite him into office (Childers, 1983).

HITLER COMES TO POWER

Yet the nature of the German political system ensured that it was the conservative elites who controlled that system who had a much greater influence over Hitler coming to power than the electors. From March 1930 to January 1933, Germany was in a perpetual state of political crisis, with all the major political decisions being taken outside the Reichstag by an inner circle of conservative advisers surrounding the elderly Hindenburg. This undemocratic and isolated grouping consisted of senior figures in the army, members of the upper echelons of the civil service, powerful Junker landowners, and some leading industrialists. All these groups had one thing in common: they wanted Weimar democracy replaced by a more authoritarian regime.

It seems that, during the early 1930s, Hindenburg was trying to establish a right-wing authoritarian regime which excluded the Nazis, as he felt they were much too unpredictable and violent to entrust with the future of Germany. In March 1930, Hindenburg appointed a 46-year-old former army officer, Heinrich Brüning, of the Catholic Centre Party, as the Chancellor of a centre-right minority 'national government' which introduced a bleak set of deflationary policies, including public expenditure cuts, salary reductions for public sector workers, tax increases, and damaging reductions in social welfare benefits. This strong medicine made the economic depression much worse and greatly increased unemployment. This economic strategy was also designed to highlight Germany's inability to pay reparations. In the end, Brüning's economic medicine, although it forced Germans to live within their means for the first time since 1918, made his government extremely unpopular and helped to sustain the gloomy economic circumstances in which the extreme parties of the left and right thrived.

As the popularity of the Brüning regime plummeted, Hitler was being increasingly courted by Alfred Hugenberg, the leader of the traditional conservative DNVP, to form a right-wing alliance. These negotiations came to nothing, primarily because Hitler refused to weaken the independence of the Nazi Party by openly associating with 'reactionary' forms of conservative nationalism. Yet Hitler continued to keep open channels of communication with Hindenburg's circle, with business leaders, and with powerful figures in the army, as he realised it was unlikely he would come to power without their agreement. In January 1932, for example, he gave an important speech to the influential Industry Club in Düsseldorf during which he claimed business had nothing to fear from a Nazi regime [*Doc. 16*]. However, the immediate response of leading business leaders to Hitler's Düsseldorf speech was very disappointing. The only major Ruhr industrialist to back the Nazis before 1933 was Fritz Thyssen. Most of the funds the Nazis received from business before they came to power came from the small business sector, not the big industrialists who continued to give the bulk of their financial support to the traditional centre-right parties. Hitler was much more successful in increasing Nazi influence within the German army. There is little doubt that among younger army officers the Nazi Party was increasingly attractive, while among the higher reaches of the officer class there was also a great deal of sympathy, if not outright support, for the Nazis.

In the spring of 1932, Hitler decided to challenge Hindenburg for the presidency. In the final ballot in April, Hindenburg polled 52.9 per cent of the votes while Hitler took 36.6 per cent; the Communist leader, Ernst Thalmann, took a mere 10.5 per cent. The election confirmed Hindenburg as the most popular politician in Germany, but it was also clear that most of his votes came from supporters of parties of the centre left. It was Adolf Hitler who had gained the votes of supporters of the centre right of the German electorate. Hindenburg remained President, but Hitler was clearly the undisputed leader of the German right, which included most of the middle and upper classes, and most of the voters of rural Germany.

In March 1932, Hindenburg decided to sack the increasingly unpopular Brüning, replacing him as Chancellor with Franz von Papen, a right-wing and reactionary member of the Catholic Centre Party who had close links to the aristocracy and the army but little parliamentary or popular support. Papen, a Catholic aristocrat and fervent nationalist from Westphalia, was dubbed by his socialist critics 'a Nazi in pin-striped suit'. He certainly acted like one by immediately declaring a state of emergency, suspending the Prussian parliament (thereby ending the power of the last stronghold of the democratic SPD), and arranging vast military parades through Berlin which echoed the militarism of the Second Reich. By now, some leading figures within the army had established informal links with the Nazi Party in an attempt to gain Nazi toleration for the new government. The deposing of the Prussian parliament, which consisted of a coalition between the SPD and the Catholic Centre Party, was a crippling blow to democracy in the Weimar Republic and quite clearly led the way towards the creation of a right-wing dictatorship.

In July 1932, Papen called a general election, which did not lead to greater support for his own party but a massive increase of support for the Nazi Party, which polled 37.3 per cent of the votes and took 230 seats in the Reichstag. Nazi gains in the election were at the expense of the right-wing nationalists and conservatives who had been supporting the Papen government. Nazi voters saw Hitler as the best insurance policy against a possible communist revolution. The Nazi Party was now the dominant force in German political life, and appeared to be sweeping all before it. Hitler's speeches had been heard by 500,000 Germans during the election campaign, and Nazi posters and banners were everywhere. Hitler, who felt he was in a very strong political position, demanded to be made Chancellor. But Hindenburg stubbornly refused to accede to the demands of the Nazi leader, and continued to exclude the Nazis from government.

The refusal of Hindenburg to appoint Hitler as Chancellor after the July 1932 election was a serious blow to the Nazi Party, which was becoming exhausted from continual campaigning and was in danger of losing energy and voters. In November 1932, sensing the Nazis were be-coming overtaxed by constant electioneering, Papen called yet another election, which saw the Nazi vote fall by 2 million and their seats in the Reichstag drop from 230 to 196. For the first time since the onset of the economic depression, Nazi electoral support had actually fallen. In spite of Hitler's remarkable achievement in unifying most of the right-wing forces in German society, the Nazi Party remained opposed by most voters of the centre left, which accounted for the majority of German electors. The steady decline of the liberal centre parties appeared to have been halted at the election of November 1932. The Nazi myth that 'tomorrow belonged to them' had been severely dented. Hitler's desire to gain power without the need of a coalition was now compromised.

Yet when Papen offered Hitler the chance to join his government, he stubbornly turned it down. He continued to insist he would only become Chancellor in a Cabinet dominated by Nazis, with the full power to rule using Article 48 of the constitution. Papen now thought the only way forward for the German right was to create a 'presidential dictatorship' which suppressed the Nazis and the communists with the support of the army. But this idea was rejected by Hindenburg as he felt it would trigger a civil war, with the Nazis and communists fighting out the future of Germany on the streets. The view of the army general staff was that their troops could not control both the communists and the Nazis at the same time.

In November 1932, the Papen regime was finally driven out of office by a vote of no confidence in the Reichstag. By now, parliamentary government had virtually ceased to exist. During 1932, the strife-ridden Reichstag met only thirteen times. This breakdown of parliamentary government was not vigorously opposed either inside or outside parliament.

Hindenburg was now coming under increasing pressure from within the army and among leading industrialists to appoint an authoritarian right-wing government with some popular support. In the conservative press, there were daily calls for the creation of a 'constitutional dictatorship' in order to get Germany out of its persistent political paralysis. The only party on the right with any popular support remained the Nazi Party. Yet Hindenburg remained unsure about placing the fate of Germany in the hands of Adolf Hitler. There were, however, many others within Hindenburg's circle, most notably Papen, who believed Hitler could be 'tamed' or 'domesticated' if he was given the awesome responsibility of power.

On 2 December 1932, Hindenburg, still ignoring Hitler's claims to lead Germany, appointed a leading army figure, General von Schleicher, as the new German Chancellor. Schleicher immediately announced the main task of the new government was to tackle unemployment. He initially hoped Hitler would give support to his government, but the Nazi leader refused to do so. To give his regime some popular legitimacy, Schleicher decided to appeal to the 'socialist' wing of the Nazi Party. He opened negotiations with leading trade unionists, and then repealed Papen's unpopular anti-trade union laws. Even more controversial was his invitation to Gregor Strasser, the leading 'socialist' Nazi, to become Vice-Chancellor. Both these initiatives came to nothing. The trade unions rejected his overtures, and Gregor Strasser was forced to resign from the Nazi Party in some disgrace.

By January 1933, Schleicher was asking Hindenburg to transform his government into a military dictatorship. But Hindenburg refused to accede to these demands, as Schleicher had no popular backing from either the left or the right. Even worse, Schleicher's economic policies, especially those aimed at workers, were causing growing alarm among leading industrialists. All Schleicher achieved was to make leading figures in industry and the army look more favourably on Hitler and the Nazis. In so many ways, therefore, Schleicher's extremely poor political judgement in courting the centre left helped make a Hitler-led government more attractive to the traditional forces of the right. This change of mood provided the environment in which Hitler was brought to power.

It was Papen, who still retained some political influence with Hindenburg, who played the most decisive backstage role in bringing Hitler to power. Papen believed Hitler could be harnessed to serve the needs of the old guard. He was also convinced that, if the right wanted to establish a popular authoritarian government, then Hitler, whose charisma was unmatched, was really the only possible leader of such a government. At the end of January 1933, a decisive meeting took place in Berlin between Hindenburg and Hitler. The President's son told his father shortly after the meeting that the Nazi leader had to be appointed Chancellor [*Doc. 20*]. It seems the conversion of his trusted son to the idea of Hitler being used to serve the interests of the nationalist right was a vital influence on Hindenburg's decision to appoint Hitler as German Chancellor on 30 January 1933 as the head of a 'national' coalition government which included only three Nazis. Hitler was 'invited' into office by Hindenburg to establish a stable and popular right-wing authoritarian dictatorship which would uphold the aims of the army, the agrarian Junkers and big business. A relatively painless counter-revolution against those who had gained from the post-1918 revolution was what was desired, and Hitler was felt to be a suitable figurehead for this new old order.

It is, of course, convincing to argue that Hitler could only have made his way through the back door of power with the help of the key power holders of the German state: the President and his close army advisers. At the same time, Hitler's political skill in exploiting the power vacuum which existed on the German right should not be underestimated. The solution of putting into power unpopular politicians or army figures, which Hindenburg, increasingly out of touch, persisted with from 1930 onwards was unsustainable. Hitler's promises to destroy the power of socialism and the trade unions, and to rebuild the German armed forces, made him a logical partner for the army in the creation of a right-wing, pro-capitalist, militaristic and protectionist regime likely to appeal to industrial capitalists and the anti-democratic forces that still dominated the higher echelons of German society. The right-wing forces in German society which systematically destroyed democracy in Germany from 1930 onwards were actually ensuring that a right-wing popular dictatorship, led by a charismatic leader, would be the inevitable outcome of their handiwork.

PART THREE

CHAPTER SEVEN

WHY DID HITLER COME TO POWER?

The rise of the Nazi Party and the factors which brought Adolf Hitler to power in January 1933 have been the subject of intense historical debate. Most studies that have examined the collapse of democracy in Germany and the rise of Nazism nearly always concentrate on the following factors: the vulnerability of the Weimar constitution; the problems created by the imposition of the 'hated' Treaty of Versailles; the deep economic problems that beset Germany, most notably the 'great inflation' and the economic slump of the early 1930s; the lack of a democratic consensus; the existence of extreme parties of the left and right who desired the overthrow of democracy; and the presence of leading figures in the army, civil service and within industry who were equally indifferent to the survival of the infant republic.

With such a vast list of seemingly insoluble problems, and given its inherent flaws, it is surprising the Weimar Republic lasted as long as it did. Yet we must not forget that it lasted longer than the Third Reich. All of the difficulties that faced Weimar democracy did not occur at one and the same time. In fact, the period 1919–23 was extremely turbulent. It could even be said that the Weimar Republic was more politically and economically unstable in that period than at any other time. But democracy survived. The period between 1924 and 1929 was one of relative economic stability, and democratic rule was never once seriously threatened. Even in the period 1929–33, when unemployment rose, Germany suffered severe economic difficulties, but there was no attempt made by any group on either the right or left to bring about an overthrow of the republic by force. It must be remembered that high unemployment, the major consequence of the depression, was higher in percentage terms in the USA and various other European countries, which did not develop fascist regimes, than in Germany, and the view that the depression brought Hitler to power is not credible, as most of the unemployed voted communist, not Nazi. When democracy collapsed, it was destroyed by a conspiracy between the power holders in government and parties of the extreme right. The decisive new ingredients in the period 1929–33 were the supreme indifference of Hindenburg and his inner circle to sustain democracy, and the growth in support for Adolf Hitler and the Nazi Party. It was the mixture of these two factors, operating at a time of economic depression, that ensured the collapse of Weimar democracy and the creation of the Third Reich.

Some historians suggest the primary blame for the destruction of democracy in Germany rests with the authoritarian right who brought the unpredictable Adolf Hitler to power in the hope that he could be tamed and, used to serve their own authoritarian, though somewhat less extreme, ends. Hitler's appointment came at the end of a crisis in the party-political state in Germany which began in 1930 with the appointment of Brüning. In truth, Hindenburg's actions in using Article 48 to sustain unrepresentative right-wing leaders and governments from 1930 onwards mortally damaged the infant democratic structure in Weimar Germany and ensured the country would have some type of authoritarian government during the 1930s. According to Alan Bullock, Hitler was 'jobbed into office' during a period when the electoral popularity of the Nazi Party was on the wane. On this view, Hitler's 'seizure of power' came about because the structure of demo-cracy in Weimar Germany was reliant on reactionary forces at a critical juncture, and they decided to destroy it, hiring Hitler and the Nazi Party in a cloak-and-dagger fashion to do their dirty work (Bullock, 1962). Other writers have viewed Hitler as the unwitting agent of the bourgeoisie, chosen to serve the same function as Napoleon had done for the French bourgeoisie over a century earlier. For Gorgi Dimitroff, Nazism was the 'open terrorist dictatorship of the most reactionary, most chauvinist, and most imperial elements of finance capital' (Kershaw, 2000: 12).

The major problem with viewing Hitler as a mere agent of the upper classes, or as the puppet of big business, is that it underestimates the role of Hitler's own personality and the political skills he exerted on events at a particular place and time, and consigns National Socialism to a historical blind alley. The desire to see the 'German tragedy' as some sort of tragic accident, or an upper-class cloak-and-dagger conspiracy gone wrong, is not surprising, given the barbarity and criminality connected with the Nazi regime and the obvious dangers of turning Hitler into some present-day hero. As Wolfgang Saur puts it: 'In Nazism the historian faces a pheno-menon that leaves him [her] no way but rejection' (Kershaw, 2000: 17). At the same time, a historian is expected to show 'sympathetic understanding' when approaching any historical subject, something which is extremely difficult when that subject is the rise of Hitler and the Nazi Party.

Yet we must not forget that, at precisely the same time as democracy was being undermined in Germany, the popularity of Hitler and the Nazi Party in democratic elections was increasing at a quite incredible rate. After 1929, Hitler was the single most dynamic politician in Germany and the most popular leader on the centre right. Nazism had the support of nearly 12 million Germans over voting age in July 1932, and of many young Germans who did not yet have the right to vote. In recent years, new research on voting behaviour has shown that the Nazi Party was not purely and simply a party of middle-class resentment, but drew support from a broader range of class groupings than any other German party. It seems the most powerful reason why these diverse groups supported Nazism was not primarily because of its opposition to the Treaty of Versailles or its anti-Semitism, but because of its utopian promise to end class-based politics and replace them with a popular, ethnically united folk community. A great part of this appeal, especially to the middle classes, but also to working-class supporters of Nazism, was a desire to weaken the power of Marxism in Germany, and to put an end to democratic government. Hitler appealed to many Germans before 1933 because he promised to achieve social harmony by the creative destruction of those groups in German society who he claimed were opponents of his vision of an ethnically united folk community.

In spite of the dangers of stressing the 'uniqueness' of Nazism and the 'peculiarities' of German history, it remains difficult to reject the view that there were certain unique aspects of German politics, culture and society in the aftermath of the crisis of the defeat in the First World War which did allow nationalism to flourish in a very distinctive manner in Germany. The dramatic changes that defeat brought about in Germany did produce feelings of isolation, frustration, insecurity, anger, which greatly affected the middle-class groups that gave support to Nazism. At the same time, it must be appreciated that the growth of mass industrial society, accompanied by the social changes brought about by the First World War, affected all of European society, and made the establishment of stable democracies very difficult to achieve anywhere, especially in countries without democratic traditions. There were many within the landed and the middle classes in Germany who disliked the class struggle championed by socialists and Marxists, and felt democracy was not strong enough to end this struggle. It is perhaps significant that the most stable European democracy in the inter-war period, Britain, which had been on the winning side in the war, remained relatively free of both fascism and Marxism, while two of the newest democracies in Europe, Italy and Germany, both collapsed and established right-wing authoritarian regimes that decided to escape from the freedom of democracy into what seemed the more simple structure of a nationalist dictatorship.

It is difficult to decide whether the rise of the Nazi Party was the public expression of an irrational and incomprehensible resistance to modern-isation (an 'escape from freedom'), or a specific German response to the creation of a modern democracy in a society without a long democratic tradition. It is worth noting that many of the hard-core supporters of

Nazism were also among the strongest opponents of Marxism, and were more often than not 'losers' in the drive towards modernity. This was especially true of the people in small towns and rural areas who supported the Nazi Party, but it was also true of many of the other supporters of the party in urban areas. Detlev Peukert argued the rise of the Nazi Party combined traditional 'conservative' values, such as the promise to restore an authoritarian system of government and a return to the land, with a desire to use modern techniques in industry for the good of the 'nation' through rearmament and more efficient use of industrial resources (Fischer, 1995: 123).

For George Mosse, Nazism was a unique revolution of the right with goals of its own, and was not a mere opportunistic movement led by a power-crazed individual without clear ideological objectives (Mosse, 1966). According to Roger Griffin, Nazism was not the agent of any other force, or the reflection of one single class, but the product of the conditions that existed in countries with powerful nationalist forces and limited experience of democratic traditions. It was not merely an attempt to stop modern-isation by simply 'turning back the clock', but offered to use a combination of modern ideas and traditional values to create a new utopia, a genuine third way between liberal democracy and socialism. Ian Kershaw has recently suggested that research on the social basis of Nazi electoral support before 1933 strongly indicates it was the dynamic and radical aspects of the Nazi programme and its support for 'modernisation' in some areas of policy that attracted as many voters as the backward-looking, often anti-scientific, negative and reactionary aspects of its election campaigns (Kershaw, 2000). Hitler never supported the desire of some radicals in the party for de-industrialisation. It must also be emphasised that the whole idea of *Lebensraum* put a high priority on exploiting raw materials and agricultural resources using modern industrial techniques. The Holocaust would do much the same. It was indeed a Nazi dream that the new Germany would combine strong industrial and agricultural sectors. The idea of creating an ethnically united new nation with unlimited freedom from international control was also a very modern idea. In fact, the Nazis promised to modernise warfare and, ultimately, genocide.

Hitler offered a utopian vision at a time of deep gloom and pessimism. He promised a new cult of leadership, a racial revolution, a utopian folk community, a new kind of racial imperialism which would make Germany the dominant power in Europe, and the end of class conflict and of all Jewish influence. Hitler may have collaborated with existing elites to achieve power, but he always promised voters that if he came to power he would create a new Germany. Even though Hitler's proposed utopia was, like all others, unrealisable, it was comforting to certain sections of German society to think about living in such a seemingly conflict-free society at a time when their society appeared conflict-ridden. Hitler also stressed that Germany's economic problems stemmed from military defeat and foreign and 'Jewish' exploitation, and that these could be solved by a vigorous Nazi dedication to restore German economic and military power.

The reason why Nazism was able to attract so many Germans after 1929 was due to the fact that democratic government, a relatively new phenomenon in Germany, was viewed with great indifference by many millions of Germans, and because the Nazi Party offered a new and appealing utopian vision. This helps to explain why Hitler was able to attract nearly 12 million Germans within a democratic system to a party dedicated to destroying that system. Another factor which unquestionably attracted voters to the Nazi Party was the existence of a genuine 'revolutionary' threat from the communist left. The KPD was as dedicated to the destruction of democracy in Germany as were the Nazis, though the KPD wanted to replace it with a communist regime. Hitler played up the 'Red menace' very strongly and presented the Nazi Party as the best insurance against a communist revolution. Many groups in German society – and they were not just capitalist businessmen or members of the reactionary 'old gang' – viewed socialism as one of the chief sources of division in Germany, and the creative destruction of socialism, which Hitler promised, was an attractive proposition during the period when Nazi popularity grew and eventually proved attractive to the power brokers who ran Germany.

What Hitler offered, above all – and this was especially important at a time of severe political tension and economic depression – was the promise of strong, clear leadership based on authoritarian principles. Many millions of Germans who turned to the Nazis did so because they found the idea of a strong leader extremely attractive. Adolf Hitler was a charismatic public speaker who moved those who heard him speak with a passion which many describe in religious terms. To deny that Hitler had this power is to fail to understand the mood in Germany during the early 1930s [*Doc. 18*]. We may not be able to comprehend Hitler's power to inspire at this place and time, and, given what came later, we may not wish to believe it ever existed. Yet to deny it existed, or to dismiss Hitler's seductive power to rouse many millions of 'ordinary' Germans, is a dereliction of analytical objectivity, and it amounts to bland fence-sitting by those who continue to dismiss Hitler's political and oratorical ability. Whatever it was about this ordinary-looking individual, he was able to inspire other ordinary individuals to feel his anger and to share his visionary dream, no matter how repulsive that dream may now appear with the benefit of hindsight and the knowledge of the gas ovens.

Hitler was faced at every turn during the early 1930s by weak and vacillating opponents. For the authoritarian right, Hitler was the only politician close enough to many of their own views who, with the aid of the mass media, stood any chance of taking his enormous body of existing supporters and establishing the popular authoritarian regime they desired. The only alternatives to Hitler coming to power were a presidential dictatorship led by Hindenburg, a return to parliamentary coalitions of the centre left, a communist revolution, or the continuation of unpopular civilian politicians ruling with the consent of Hindenburg. Of these options, the only one Hindenburg considered was to continue with an authoritarian regime led by a politician he controlled. The only other alternative was a communist revolution, but the communists were not well armed enough, nor popular enough, to have defeated the armed forces and established a viable government.

In the end, Hindenburg accepted a logic that had been pressed upon him by many leading figures in his entourage ever since 1930, namely, that Hitler should be brought into government, hopefully shackled, controlled, and then utilised to serve the old guard. This was, of course, a monumental error of political judgement, as Hitler had always proclaimed both publicly and privately his determination, if he came to power legally, to destroy the constitution and set up a dictatorship. Whether such an incredible force as Adolf Hitler would have just disappeared from the scene had Hindenburg not brought him to power in January 1933 appears extremely unlikely. Of course, Hitler might have abandoned the 'legal path to power' and returned to the streets armed with the full knowledge that the army was keen to deal with the 'communist menace' and wanted unlimited funds for rearmament. The only viable popular leader for an authoritarian, militaristic regime, which Germany's political, business and military rulers all wanted, was Adolf Hitler, and it would have been a miracle, given the nature of German politics in early 1933, if he had not come to power.

PART FOUR   DOCUMENTS

DOCUMENT 1   HITLER IN VIENNA

One of Hitler's closest friends as a young person was August Kubizek, who spent some time with the future Nazi dictator in Vienna. In this document, Kubizek offers some observations on Hitler's views of the ethnic diversity of Viennese life:

When home-going workers passed us by, Adolf would grip my arm and say, 'Did you hear, Gustl? Czechs!'. Another time, we encountered some bricklayers speaking loudly in Italian, with florid gestures. 'There you have your German Vienna,' he cried, indignantly. This, too, was one of his oft repeated phrases: 'German Vienna', but Adolf pronounced it with a bitter undertone ... He hated the babel in the streets of Vienna, this 'incest incarnate' as he called it later. He hated this State, which ruined Germanism, and the pillars that supported this State: the reigning house, the Church, the nobility, the capitalists and the Jews ... His accumulated hatred of all forces which threatened the Germans was mainly concentrated upon the Jews, who played a leading role in Vienna.

A. Kubizek, *Young Hitler: The Story of our Friendship* (London: Macmillan, 1954), pp. 185–6.

DOCUMENT 2   HITLER'S FIRST APPEARANCE AT A MEETING OF THE GERMAN WORKERS' PARTY, 12 SEPTEMBER 1919

In the following document, Anton Drexler, the leader of the German Workers' Party (DAP), describes his first impression of Adolf Hitler, at a party meeting:

On 12 September 1919, the German Workers' Party held a monthly meeting in the Veterans' Hall of the Sterneckerbrau ... The first National Socialist pamphlet, *My Political Awakening* ... had just appeared. I had collected a few proof copies from my publisher, Dr. Boepple, and was standing with five copies in my hand at the bar of the pub, listening with growing enthusiasm to the second speaker in the evening's discussion, who was a guest. He was dealing with the first speaker in the discussion, a Professor Baumann, who had urged the secession of Bavaria from Germany, and he was tackling the Professor in a way that was a joy to watch. He had a short but trenchant speech in favour of a greater Germany which thrilled me and all who could hear him. When the speaker finished I rushed towards him, thanked him for what he had said and asked him to take the pamphlet I had away with him to read. It contained, I said, the rules and basic ideas of the new movement; if he was in agreement with them, he could come again in a week's time and work in a smaller circle, because we could do with people like him.

J. Noakes and G. Pridham, *Nazism, 1919–1945*. Vol 1: *The Rise to Power, 1919–1934*

(Exeter: University of Exeter Press, 1983), p. 11.

DOCUMENT 3　**THE 25 POINTS OF THE NAZI PARTY PROGRAMME**

The Nazi Party programme, announced on 25 February 1920, remained the key rallying point for party members before 1933.

1.　We demand the union of all Germans to form a Greater Germany on the basis of the right of self-determination enjoyed by nations.

2.　We demand equality of rights for the German people in its dealings with other nations and abolition of the peace treaties of Versailles and Saint Germain.

3.　We demand land and territory (colonies) for the nourishment of our people and for settling our excess population.

4.　None but members of the nation may be citizens of the state. None but those of German blood, whatever their creed, may be members of the nation. No Jew therefore may be a member of the nation.

5.　Anyone who is not a citizen of the state may live in Germany only as a guest and must be regarded as being subject to foreign laws.

6.　The right of voting on the leadership and legislation is to be enjoyed by the state alone. We demand therefore that all official appointments, of whatever kind, whether in the Reich, in the country, or in the smaller localities, shall be granted to citizens of the state alone. We oppose Parliament's corrupting custom of filling posts merely with a view to party considerations and without reference to character or capacity.

7.　We demand that the state shall make it its first duty to promote the industry and livelihood of citizens of the state. If it is not possible to nourish the entire population of the state, foreign nationals (noncitizens of the state) must be excluded from the Reich.

8.　All non-German immigration must be prevented.

9.　All citizens of the state shall be equal as regards rights and duties.

10.　It must be the first duty of each citizen of the state to work with his mind or with his body. The activities of the individual may not clash with the interests of the whole, but must proceed within the frame of the community and be for the general good.

We demand therefore:

11.　Abolition of incomes unearned by work.

12.　In view of the enormous sacrifice of life and property demanded of a nation by every war, personal enrichment due to a war must be regarded as a crime against the nation. We demand therefore ruthless confiscation of all war gains.

13. We demand nationalisation of all business trusts.

14. We demand that the profits from the wholesale trade shall be shared.

15. We demand extensive development of security for old age.

16. We demand creation and maintenance of a healthy middle class, immediate communisation of wholesale business premises, and their lease at a cheap rate to small traders, and that extreme consideration shall be shown to all small purveyors to the state, district authorities and smaller localities.

17. We demand land reform suitable to our national requirements.

18. We demand ruthless prosecution of those whose activities are injurious to the common interest. Sordid criminals against the nation, usurers, profiteers, etc., must be punished by death, whatever their creed or race.

19. We demand that the Roman Law, which serves the materialistic world order, shall be replaced by a legal system for all Germany.

20. With the aim of opening to every capable and industrious German the possibility of higher education and of thus obtaining advancement, the state must consider a thorough reconstruction of our national system of education.

21. The state must see to raising the standard of health in the nation by protecting mothers and infants, prohibiting child labour, incising bodily efficiency by obligatory gymnastics and sports laid down by law, and by extensive support of clubs engaged in the bodily development of the young.

22. We demand the abolition of a paid army and formation of a national popular army.

23. We demand legal warfare against conscious political lying and its dissemination in the press. In order to facilitate creation of a German national press we demand:

(a) that all editors and their assistants of newspapers employing the German language must be members of the nation;

(b) that special permission from the state shall be necessary before non-German newspapers can appear. These are not necessarily printed in the German language;

(c) that non-Germans shall be prohibited by law from participating financially in or influencing German newspapers ... It must be forbidden to publish papers which do not promote the national welfare. We demand legal prosecution of tendencies in art and literature of a kind likely to disintegrate our life as a nation, and the suppression of institutions which militate against the requirements mentioned above.

24. We demand liberty for all religious denominations in the state, so far as they are not a danger to it and do not militate against moral feelings of the

German race. The party as such stands for positive Christianity, but does not bind itself in the matter of creed to any particular confession. It combats the Jewish-materialist spirit within us and outside us.

25. That all the foregoing may be realised, we demand the creation of a strong central power in the state. Unquestioned authority of the politically centralised Parliament over the entire Reich and its organisations and formation of chambers for classes and occupations for the purpose of carrying out the general laws promulgated by the Reich in the various states of the confederation.

The leaders of the party swear to go straight forward – if necessary, to sacrifice their lives – in securing the fulfilment of the foregoing points.

Nazi Party programme, 1920.

DOCUMENT 4   THE DEMANDS OF THE NAZI PARTY

In this document, Hitler outlines some of the key demands of the Nazi Party:

1. We must call to account the November criminals of 1918. It cannot be that two million Germans should have fallen in vain and afterwards one should sit down as friends at the same table with traitors. No, we do not pardon, we demand – Vengeance!

2. The dishonouring of the nation must cease. For the betrayers of their Fatherland and informers the gallows is the proper place. Our streets and squares shall once more bear the names of our heroes; they shall not be named after Jews. In the Question of Guilt we must proclaim the truth.

3. The administration of the state must be cleared of the rabble which is fattened at the state of the parties.

4. The present laxity in the fight against usury must be abandoned. Here the punishment is the same as that for the betrayers of their Fatherland.

5. We must demand a great enlightenment on the subject of the peace treaty. With thoughts of love? No! But in holy hatred against those who have ruined us.

6. The lies which veil from us our misfortunes must cease. The fraud of the present money madness must be shown up.

7. As the foundation for a new currency, the property of those who are not of our blood will be used. If families who have lived in Germany for a thousand years are now expropriated, we must do the same to the Jewish usurers.

8. We demand the immediate expulsion of all Jews who have entered Germany since 1914, and all those too, who through the trickery of the stock exchange or through other shady transactions have gained their wealth.

9. The housing scarcity must be relieved through energetic action; houses must be granted to those who deserve them.

Hitler speech, 18 September 1922, quoted in N. Baynes, *The Speeches of Adolf Hitler*, vol. 1 (Oxford: Oxford University Press, 1942), pp. 107–8.

DOCUMENT 5   HITLER ON THE LEADERSHIP PRINCIPLE

The idea of total authority being invested in the leader of the Nazi Party was established in 1921, and became a key aspect of the organisation of the party thereafter. In this document, Adolf Hitler explains the origin of the leadership principle:

In the years 1920–21 the movement had a committee in control of it, elected by the members in assembly. This committee, comically enough, embodied the very principle which the movement was most keenly fighting, namely, parliamentarianism. I refused to countenance such folly, and after a very short time I ceased to attend the meetings of the committee. I made my propaganda as I wished, and that was the end of it … As soon as the new rules were adopted and I was established as Chairman of the party, thus acquiring the necessary authority and the rights accompanying it, all such folly came to an immediate end. Decisions by committee were replaced by the principle of absolute responsibility. The chairman is responsible for entire control of the movement.

The principle gradually became recognised inside the movement as a natural one, at least as far as control of the party was concerned.

A. Hitler, *Mein Kampf* (London: Paternoster, 1938), pp. 234–5.

DOCUMENT 6   THE MUNICH BEER HALL PUTSCH

In this document, Herr Muller, a historian who was in the Bürgerbraukeller, provides an eyewitness account of the Munich Beer Hall Putsch:

Herr von Kahr had spoken for half an hour. Then there was a movement at the entrance as if people were wanting to push their way in. Despite several warnings, the disturbance did not die down. Herr von Kahr had to break off speaking. Eventually, steel helmets came into sight. From this moment on, the view from my seat was rather obscured. People stood on chairs so that I didn't see Hitler until he had come fairly near along the main gangway; just before he turned to the platform. I saw him emerge between two armed soldiers in steel helmets who carried pistols next to their heads, pointing at the ceiling. They turned towards the platform. Hitler climbed on to a chair to my left … Thereupon Hitler called out … 'The National

Revolution has broken out. The hall is surrounded' ... The gentlemen did not move. The General State Commissioner [Kahr] had stepped back and stood back and stood opposite him, looking at him calmly. Then Hitler went towards the platform. What happened I could not see exactly. I heard him talk to the gentlemen and I heard the words: Everything would be over in ten minutes if the gentlemen would go with him. To my surprise, the three gentlemen [Kahr, Lossow and Seisser] went out with him immediately ... The general mood – I can of course only judge from my surroundings, but I think that this represented the general feeling in the hall – was still against the whole business ... The change came only during Hitler's second speech when he entered about ten minutes later, went to the platform and made a short speech. It was a rhetorical masterpiece. In fact, in a few sentences it totally transformed the mood of the audience. I have rarely seen anything like it ... An hour after Hitler's first appearance, the three gentlemen [Kahr, Lossow and Seisser] came back into the hall, with Hitler and Ludendorff. They were enthusiastically received. On the platform Kahr began to speak first without being requested to and gave the speech which was printed word for word in the papers. Ludendorff spoke without being requested to, whereas Lossow and Seisser only spoke after repeated requests ... If I am to depict the impression made by the gentleman on the platform, I would say Kahr was completely unmoved. His face was like a mask all evening. He was not pale or agitated, he was very serious, but spoke very composedly. I got the impression that there was a melancholy look in his eyes. But that is perhaps being subjective. Hitler, on the other hand, was radiant with joy. One had the feeling that he was delighted to have succeeded in persuading Kahr to collaborate. There was in his demeanor, I would say, a kind of childhood joy, a very frank expression which I will never forget.

J. Noakes and G. Pridham, *Nazism, 1919–1945*, Vol. 1: *The Rise to Power, 1919–1934* (Exeter: University of Exeter Press, 1983), pp. 28–9, 32.

DOCUMENT 7   HITLER ON THE KEY LESSON OF THE MUNICH BEER HALL PUTSCH

In the following document, taken from a speech given by Hitler in 1936, the Nazi leader explains the importance of the failure in 1923 to the subsequent history of the Nazi Party:

From the failure of the Putsch we drew a great lesson for the future ... And so only a few days after the collapse I formed a new decision; that now without any haste the conditions must be created which would exclude the possibility of another failure ... The experience of 1923 produced later the miracle that we could effect a revolution without in the least disturbing domestic order or bringing the life of our people in danger ... We have conquered our State without, I believe, the breaking of a single window pane. This was possible only thanks to thorough preparation and the building up of the Party ... And the greatest miracle of all; it is perhaps due solely to the experience of 1923 that we were able to sail round the rock which faces any revolution such as ours, viz., the problem of our relation to the existing so-called 'legal instruments of power' of the state.

Hitler speech, September 1936, quoted in N. Baynes, *The Speeches of Adolf Hitler*, vol. 1
(Oxford: Oxford University Press, 1942), pp. 155–8.

DOCUMENT 8   JOSEPH GOEBBELS'S VIEWS ON NATIONAL SOCIALISM

In this document, from the mid-1920s Joseph Goebbels outlines differences between National Socialism and Marxist and liberal nationalist parties:

There are people in our camp, not the worst ones, who learned something after 1918 and are therefore still learning after 1923. Today they see not only the falsification of the socialist idea in Marxism, but also, just as clearly and plainly, the falsification of nationalism in the so-called national parties and organisations of every hue. They are prepared to draw from these insights the necessary political conclusions. They turn just as sharply against middle-class views as against Marxist proletarian ones ... For them, the middle class, in its political organisations, has lost the right to take a stand against any consequence of the politics of this system just as much as has Marxism, because both are guilty of this system, because both have participated in this system and will continue to do so, whenever and wherever the stampede to the fodder trough permits it. Down with the madness of Marxism, for it is falsified socialism! Down with the madness of the so-called nationalist opposition in the parties of the right! For it is falsified nationalism. These are the slogans which make socialism into nationalism and nationalism into socialism. For us any nationalist demand requires a socialist one; any radicalisation of the national will for freedom a radicalisation of socialism. You consistently confuse system and person. But it is always the system itself which is in question, never its temporary supporters.

J. Goebbels, 'The Radicalisation of Socialism', quoted in B. Miller Lane and J. Leila (eds.),
Nazi Ideology before 1933: A Documentation (Manchester: Manchester University Press,
1978), pp. 79–80.

DOCUMENT 9   HITLER ON THE POWER OF THE SPOKEN WORD

In this extract from Mein Kampf, Hitler explains the unique emotional power of the spoken word:

All great, world shaking events have been brought about not by written matter but by the spoken word … The bourgeois intelligentsia protest against such a view only because they themselves obviously lack the power and ability to influence the masses by the spoken word, since they have thrown themselves more and more into purely literary activity, and renounced the real agitational activity of the spoken word. Such habits necessarily lead in time to what distinguishes our bourgeoisie today; that is, the loss of the psychological instinct for mass effect and mass influence.

While the speaker gets a continuous correction of his speech from the crowd he is addressing – since he can always see in the faces of his listeners to what extent they can follow his arguments with understanding and whether the impression and the effect of his words lead to the desired goal – the writer does not know his readers at all. Therefore, to begin with, he will not aim at a definite mass before his eyes but will keep his arguments entirely general. By this to a certain degree he loses psychological subtlety and in consequence suppleness. And so by and large a brilliant speaker will be able to write better than a brilliant writer can speak, unless he continuously practises this art. On top of this there is the fact that the mass of the people as such is lazy; that they remain inertly in the spirit of their old habits and, left to themselves, will take up a piece of written matter only reluctantly if it is not in agreement with what they themselves believe and does not bring them what they had hoped for … The essential point, however, is that a piece of literature never knows into what hands it will fall and yet it must retain its definite form. In general the effect will be the greater, the more this form corresponds to the intellectual level and nature of those very people who will be its readers. A book that is destined for the broad masses must therefore attempt from the very beginning to have an effect, both in style and elevation, different from a work intended for the higher intellectual classes.

Only by this kind of adaptability does written matter approach the written word. To my mind, the speaker can treat the same theme as the book; he will, if he is a brilliant popular orator, not be likely to repeat the same reproach and the same substance twice in the same form. He will always let himself be borne by the great masses in such a way that instinctively the very words come to his lips that he needs to speak to the hearts of his audience. And if he errs, even in the slightest, he has the living correction before him.

As I have said, he can read from the facial expressions of his audience whether, firstly, they understand what he is saying, whether, secondly, they can follow the speech as a whole, and to what extent, thirdly, he has convinced them of the soundness of what he has said. If firstly he sees that they do not understand him, he will become so primitive and clear in his explanations that even the last member of the audience has to understand him; if he feels secondly that they do not follow him, he will construct his ideas so cautiously and slowly that even the weakest member of the audience is not left behind, and he will thirdly, if he suspects that they do not seem convinced of the soundness of his argument, repeat it over and over in constantly new examples. He himself will utter their objections, which he senses though unspoken, and go on contradicting them and exploding them until at length even the last group of an opposition, by its very beginning and facial expressions, enables him to recognise its capitulation to his arguments.

A. Hitler, *Mein Kampf*, vol. 2 (London: Paternoster, 1938), pp. 525–36.

DOCUMENT 10   THE NAZI PARTY AND PRIVATE PROPERTY

The anti-capitalist elements of the Nazi Party led to criticism from political opponents that the party would introduce 'socialist' measures if it won power. In April 1928, Hitler attempted to ease these worries by clarifying the Nazi position on private property:

In view of the false interpretations on the part of our opponents of Point 17 of the programme of the NSDAP, it is necessary to make the following statement:

Since the NSDAP accepts the principle of private property, it is self-evident that the phrase 'confiscation without compensation' refers only to the creation of possible means of confiscation, when necessary, of land acquired illegally or not managed in the public interest. It is, therefore, aimed primarily against Jewish companies which speculate on land.

J. Noakes and G. Pridham, *Nazism, 1919–1945.* Vol. 1: *The Rise to Power, 1919–1934* (Exeter: University of Exeter Press, 1983), p. 61.

DOCUMENT 11   HITLER DEBATES THE MEANING OF 'SOCIALISM' WITH OTTO STRASSER

After 1928, the Nazi Party attempted to downplay the 'socialist' parts of the party programme in order to attract votes from the middle classes and people in rural areas. Otto Strasser and other leading radicals were alarmed by this new emphasis. The following document is taken from an interview between Strasser and Adolf Hitler in 1930 in which the issue of 'socialism' was discussed:

Hitler: 'I was once an ordinary working man. I would not allow my chauffeur to eat worse than I eat myself. But your kind of socialism is nothing but Marxism. The mass of the working classes want nothing but bread and games. They will never understand the meaning of an ideal, and we cannot hope to win them over to one. What we have to do is to select from a new master class men who will not allow themselves to be guided, like you, by the morality of pity. Those who rule must know they have the right to rule because they belong to a superior race. They must maintain that right and ruthlessly consolidate it ... What you preach is liberalism, nothing but liberalism. There is only one kind of revolution, and it is not political or social, but racial, and it will always be the same: the struggle of inferior classes and races against the superior races who are in the saddle. On the day the superior race forgets this law, it is lost. All revolutions – and I have studied them carefully – have been racial ...'

Otto Strasser: 'Let us assume, Herr Hitler, that you come to power tomorrow. What would you do about Krupp's [a leading German arms company]? Would you leave it alone or not?'

Hitler: 'Of course I would leave it alone ... Do you think me so crazy as to want to ruin Germany's great industry?'

Otto Strasser: 'If you wish to preserve the capitalist regime, Herr Hitler, you have no right to talk of socialism. For our supporters are socialists, and your programme demands the socialisation of private enterprise.'

Hitler: 'That word "socialism" is the trouble ... I have never said that all enterprises should be socialised. On the contrary, I have maintained that we might socialise enterprises prejudiced to the interests of the nation. Unless they are so guilty, I should consider it a crime to destroy essential elements in our economic life. Take Italian Fascism. Our National Socialist state, like the Fascist state, will safeguard both employers' and workers' interests while reserving the right of arbitration in case of dispute. There is no reason for granting the workers a share in the profits of the enterprises that employ them, and more particularly for giving them the right to be consulted ...'

J. Noakes and G. Pridham, *Nazism, 1919–1945. Vol. 1: The Rise to Power, 1919–1934* (Exeter: University of Exeter Press, 1983), pp. 66–7.

DOCUMENT 12   HITLER DEFINES NATIONAL SOCIALISM

In the following document, taken from an article by Adolf Hitler in the Daily Express, published on 28 September 1930, the Nazi leader defines National Socialism:

'Nationalist' … I define as one to whom duty to country or community comes before self interest; in other words, 'One for all' … 'Socialist'. I define from the word 'social' meaning in the main 'social equity'. A Socialist is one who serves the common good without giving up his individuality … Our adopted term 'Socialist' has nothing to do with Marxist Socialism. Marxism is anti property; true socialism is not. Marxism places no value on the individual or individual effort, or efficiency; true Socialism values the individual and encourages him in individual efficiency, at the same time holding that his interests as an individual must be in consonance with those of the community.

Daily Express (28 September 1930).

DOCUMENT 13   THE APPEAL OF NATIONAL SOCIALISM: A PACIFIST VIEW

In this document, Heinrich Mann, a democrat and pacifist, writing in December 1931, offers his explanation for the growth of support for the Nazi Party:

It is already evening in Germany, if not midnight. That gives Mr. Hitler his big chance, as he most likely knows. Were Germans able to examine their situation with a clear head, he would not win them over … The condition of Germany is above all a psychological fact. All external facts pale in comparison. The collapse of the economy would have been nothing unusual. The economy is collapsing everywhere, but only in Germany does the process achieve its maximum effect on spirits. One recalls that the currency in all countries was threatened. Only in Germany did it succumb utterly to ruin [in 1923]; the Germans let it become ruined without any external necessity, for reasons of spirit, from a deficiency of inner resistance. Thus it could be that they now allow National Socialism to come to power because they are hearing once again the call from the abyss. The Germans hear it quite frequently. The question is whether this time they will really listen to the call from the abyss. The catastrophes they have previously suffered, after all, have taught them well …

Speaking for the victory of National Socialism, above all, is the fact that in this country democracy has never won in bloody battle. In one historical moment, after the defeat in the war, it appeared as a possible way out, compared to the disaster of the monarchy and the threat of Bolshevism – only a way out, not a goal, much less a passionate experience ... Now one sees that the state is treating Hitler's private army not as a threat to its own existence but as a desirable ally to increase its own power ... Enough – these and other circumstances as well, including the power of money, speaks for the victory of National Socialism.

H. Mann, 'Die deutsche Entscheidung', *Das Tagebuch*, vol. 12, no. 51 (19 December 1931), pp. 1964–7.

DOCUMENT 14   THE NAZI APPEAL TO FARMERS

During the early 1930s, the Nazi Party enjoyed a remarkable surge of voter support from farming communities. The following document is taken from a Nazi electoral pamphlet aimed at the German farmer and distributed prior to the July 1932 election:

German Farmer You Belong to Hitler! Why?

The German farmer stands between two great dangers today:

The one danger is the American economic system; Big Capitalism!
it means 'world economic crisis'
it means 'eternal interest slavery'
it means that the world is nothing more than a bag of booty for Jewish finance in Wall Street, New York and Paris
it enslaves man under slogans of progress, technology, rationalisation, standardisation, etc.
it knows only profits and dividends
it wants to make the world into a giant trust
it puts machine over man
it annihilates the independent, earth-rooted farmer, and its final aim is the world dictatorship of Jewry.
it achieves this in the political sphere, through parliament and the swindle of democracy. In the economic sphere, through the control of credit, the mortgaging of land, the stock exchange and the market principle
The farmer's leagues, the Landvolk, and the Bavarian Farmers' League all pay homage to this system.

The other danger is the Marxist economic system of Bolshevism:
it knows only the state economy
it knows only one class, the proletariat

it brings in controlled economy

it doesn't just annihilate the self-sufficient farmer economically – it roots him out

it brings in the rule of the tractor

it nationalises the land and creates mammoth factory-farms

it uproots and destroys man's soul, making him the powerless tool of the communist idea – or kills him

it destroys the family, belief and customs

it is anti Christ, it desecrates the churches

its final aim is the world dictatorship of the proletariat, that means ultimately the world dictatorship of Jewry, for the Jew controls this powerless proletariat and uses it for his dark plans

Big capitalism and bolshevism work hand in hand; they are born of Jewish thought and serve the master plan of world Jewry.

Who alone can rescue the farmer from these dangers?

NATIONAL SOCIALISM

'German Farmer You Belong to Hitler! Why?', National Socialist pamphlet, 1932.

DOCUMENT 15   A SCHOOLTEACHER DESCRIBES THE ATMOSPHERE AT A NAZI PARTY MEETING IN 1932

In the following document a Hamburg schoolteacher, Luise Solmitz, describes the atmosphere at a Nazi Party rally attended by Adolf Hitler in 1932:

The April sun shone hot like in summer and turned everything into a picture of gay expectation. There was immaculate order and discipline ... The hours passed, the sun shone, expectations rose ... It was nearly 3 p.m. 'The Führer is coming!' A ripple went through the crowds. Around the speaker's platform one could see hands raised in the Hitler salute. A speaker opened the meeting, abused the 'system', nobody listened to him. A second speaker welcomed Hitler and made way for the man who had drawn 120,000 people of all classes and ages. There stood Hitler in a simple black coat and looked over the crowd, waiting – a forest of swastika pennants were raised, the jubilation of this moment was given vent in a roaring salute. Main theme: 'Out of parties shall grow a nation, the German nation ... Thirteen years ago I was a simple unknown soldier. I went my way. I never turned back. Nor shall I turn back now.' Otherwise he made no personal attacks, nor any promises, vague or definite.

J. Noakes and G. Pridham, *Nazism, 1919–1945. Vol. 1: The Rise to Power, 1919–1934* (Exeter: University of Exeter Press, 1983), p. 74.

DOCUMENT 16 HITLER'S SPEECH TO THE DÜSSELDORF INDUSTRY CLUB, 27 JANUARY 1932

During 1932, Adolf Hitler attempted to cultivate support from leading figures in German industry. The following document is part of the text of Hitler's important speech to the German Industry Club in Düsseldorf on 27 January 1932:

Today we stand at the turning point of Germany's destiny. If the present development continues, Germany will one day of necessity land in Bolshevik chaos, but if this development is broken, then our people must be taken into a school of iron discipline ... A hard schooling, but one we cannot escape!

People say to me so often: 'You are the only drummer of national Germany.' And supposing that I were the only drummer? It would today be a far more statesmanlike achievement to drum once more into this German people a new faith than gradually to squander the only faith they have. Take the case of a fortress, imagine that it is reduced to extreme privations; as long as the garrison sees a possible salvation, believes in it, hopes for it, then they can bear reduced ration. But take from the hearts of men their last belief in the hope of salvation, in a better future – take that completely from them, and you will see how these men suddenly regard reduced rations as the most important thing in life.

... I know quite well, gentlemen, that when National Socialists march through the streets and suddenly in the evening a tumult and commotion arises, then the bourgeoisie draws back the window-curtain, looks out and says, 'Once more my night's rest disturbed; no more sleep for me. Why must the Nazis always be so provocative and run about the place at night?' Gentlemen, if everyone thought like that, then no one's sleep at night would be disturbed, it is true, but then the bourgeois today could not venture into the street. If everyone thought in that way, if these young folk had no ideal to move them and drive them forward, then certainly they would gladly be rid of these nocturnal nights ... Believe me, there is already in all this the force of an ideal – a great ideal. And if the whole of Germany today had the same faith in its vocation as these hundred thousands, if the whole nation possessed this idealism, Germany would stand in the world otherwise than it stands now ...

And so in contrast to our own official government I cannot see any hope for the resurrection of Germany if we regard the foreign politics of Germany as the primary factor; the primary necessity is the restoration of a sound German body politic armed to strike. In order to realise this ideal I founded thirteen years ago the National Socialist movement; that movement I have led during the last twelve years and I hope that one day it will accomplish this task and that, as the fairest result of its struggle, it will leave behind it a German body politic completely renewed internally, intolerant of anyone who sins against the nation and its interests, intolerant of anyone who will not acknowledge its vital interests or who opposes them, intolerant and pitiless against anyone who shall attempt once more to destroy or disintegrate this body politic. And yet ready for friendship and peace with anyone who has a wish for peace and friendship.

A. Kaes, M. Jay and E. Dimedberg (eds.), *The Weimar Republic Sourcebook* (Berkeley: University of California Press, 1994), pp. 138–41

DOCUMENT 17 **EDGAR JUNG ON THE 'CONSERVATIVE REVOLUTION'**

In this document, Edgar Jung, a leading Conservative journalist, describes the change in attitudes in Germany during 1932:

We currently find ourselves in the midst of a German revolution that can scarcely be expected to manifest itself in such forms as the French did through the storming of the Bastille. It will be protracted like the Reformation, but it will still leave its mark all the more fundamentally on the countenance of humanity. It will prompt a ruthless revision of all human values and dissolve all mechanical forms. It will oppose the driving intellectual forces, the formulas and the goals born of the French revolution. It will be the great conservative revolution that puts an end to occidental humanity, founding a new order, a new ethos and a new unity in the West under German leadership … The language of the German revolution will be … a world language. In the struggle for our self preservation we will, for the first time, speak a language that captures the hearts of other peoples … It is possible to maintain that it is necessary for National Socialism to be permeated by the spiritual renaissance with which Germany has been blessed in the last decade. Yet it is permissible to attribute a more limited historical task to National Socialism, the destruction of a rotten world and the preparation of the great field upon which the new seed is to be sown. This much is certain: the longing of all the masses making sacrifices today for National Socialism springs from the great conservative genetic inheritance that stirs within them and compels them to such action. Whether – to continue in the language of racial hygiene – the phenomenal form of this longing which goes today under the name of National Socialism, predominantly bears the traits of the conservative revolution or the liquidation of liberalism … The mighty energies that pulse through the German people are indestructible … That is why our hour has come: the hour of the German revolution.

E. Jung, 'Deutschland und die Konservative Revolution', in *Deutsche über Deutschland* (Munich: Albert Langen, 1932), pp. 369–82.

DOCUMENT 18   'HOW DO WE STRUGGLE AGAINST A THIRD
REICH?': THE VIEWS OF A GERMAN NOVELIST

*In this document, written in 1931, Lion Feuchtwanger, a popular novelist
from the Weimar era, offers concerns about a Germany led by Adolf Hitler:*

The war liberated the barbarian instincts of the individual and society to a
degree that was previously unimaginable. National Socialism has skilfully
organised the barbarity. Among the intellectuals it is called OBG: Organised
Barbarity of Germany.

Anti-logical and anti-intellectual in its being and ideology, National
Socialism strives to depose reason and install in its place emotion and drive
– to be precise, barbarity. Just because intellect and art are transnational,
National Socialism distrusts and hates them to the extreme. To gag the
intellect and art is one of the most important parts of its programme and
since it proclaims that they can be accomplished with the least danger, it is
here that it has its greatest success.

As National Socialism has risen in influence, it has turned with a
particular fanaticism against everything intellectual and everything artistic.
Nearly without a struggle the liberal bourgeoisie has cleared all cultural
positions for its advance. Aside from a couple of workers' theatres, no
cinema, nor theatre dares any longer to portray material hostile to the
National Socialists ... Not for a century has the mind in Germany been so
unfree as it is today.

What the intellectuals and artists have therefore to expect once the Third
Reich is definitely established is clear: extermination. And that is what the
majority does expect. Those intellectuals who can do so are already
preparing to emigrate. Anyone who moves among intellectuals in Berlin
gets the impression that Berlin is a city full of future émigrés.

It is therefore the demand of naked self-preservation that all intellectuals
struggle with body and soul and all their abilities against the Third Reich.
As long as there remains a single corner in Germany where art is allowed to
open its mouth, we want to pronounce it unmistakably and hammer it
through the skull: the Third Reich means the extermination of science, of
art, and of the intellect.

A. Kaes, M. Jay and E. Dimedberg (eds.), *The Weimar Republic Sourcebook* (Berkeley:
University of California Press, 1994), p. 167.

DOCUMENT 19   JOSEPH GOEBBELS INSTRUCTS PARTY WORKERS TO TONE DOWN 'RADICAL' ASPECTS OF THE NAZI PROGRAMME

In the following document, Joseph Goebbels instructs party workers not to attack business:

In every political situation we must adhere to the old, tried guidelines of National Socialism, not treating all business alike in the Marxist way, but distinguishing strictly between healthy business leadership, which is indispensable to the economy and exploiters. To talk of expropriation of all industrial concerns is, of course, a direct contravention of National Socialist principles.

J. Noakes and G. Pridham, *Nazism, 1919–45*. Vol. 1: *The Rise to Power, 1919–1934* (Exeter: University of Exeter Press, 1983), pp. 107–8.

DOCUMENT 20   COUNTDOWN TO HITLER COMING TO POWER

In the following document, Joachim von Ribbentrop, a young member of the Nazi Party, describes, in note form, the negotiations which led to Hitler coming to power in January 1933:

Wednesday 18 January: Hitler insists on being Chancellor. Papen again considers this impossible. His influence with Hindenburg was not strong enough to effect this. Hitler makes no further arrangements for talks …

Sunday 22 January: Hitler talks alone to young Hindenburg for two hours, followed by Hitler–Papen talk. Papen will now press for Hitler as Chancellor, but tells Hitler that he will withdraw from these negotiations forthwith if Hitler has no confidence in him …

Monday 23 January: In the morning Papen saw Hindenburg, who refused everything …

Wednesday 25 January: Hitler's Chancellorship under the auspices of a national front does not appear quite hopeless. Young Hindenburg promises to talk to Joachim again before his father makes final decision …

Friday 27 January: Hitler back in Berlin. Long talk with him at Göring's flat … Hitler declares that he has said all he wants to say to the Field Marshal [Hindenburg] and does not know what to add. Joachim persuades Hitler that this last attempt should be made, and that the situation is by no means hopeless … I have never seen Hitler in such a state; I proposed to him and Göring that I should see Papen alone that evening and explain the whole situation to him. In the evening I saw Papen and convinced him eventually that the only thing that made sense was Hitler's Chancellorship and that he must do what he can to bring this about ...

Saturday 28 January: About 11 a.m. I went to see Papen who received me with the question: 'Where is Hitler?' I told him that he had probably left, but could perhaps be contacted in Weimar. Papen said that he had to get back without delay: a turning point had been reached; after a long talk with Hindenburg, he, Papen, considered Hitler's Chancellorship possible ...

Sunday 29 January: At 11 a.m. long Hitler–Papen talk. Hitler declared that on the whole everything was clear. But there would have to be general elections and an Enabling Law. Papen saw Hindenburg immediately. I lunched with Hitler at the Kaiserhof. We discussed the elections. As Hindenburg does not want these, Hitler asked me to tell the President that these would be the last elections. In the afternoon Göring and I went to Papen. Papen declared that all obstacles are removed and that Hindenburg expects Hitler tomorrow at 11 a.m. [to appoint him as Chancellor].

Monday 30 January: Hitler appointed Chancellor.

J. Noakes and G. Pridham, *Nazism, 1919–1945. Vol. 1: The Rise to Power, 1919–1934* (Exeter: University of Exeter Press, 1983), pp. 118–20.

GLOSSARY OF TERMS AND ORGANISATIONS

Deutsche Arbeiterpartei (DAP)   The German Workers' Party, founded by Anton Drexler, a Munich locksmith. It was this party which Hitler joined and which later became the Nazi Party.

Deutsch-Nationale Volkspartei (DNVP)   The German National People's Party, the leading conservative party in Weimar Germany. This party moved to the extreme right during the early 1930s and was keen to ally with the Nazis, something that Hitler resisted. The DNVP voted for the Enabling Act in 1933 which set up Hitler's dictatorship.

Freikorps   Free Corps, the paramilitary units composed of ex-soldiers which sprang up throughout Germany after 1918. This group of former soldiers helped the nationalist right to deal with the communist threat in the immediate aftermath of the First World War.

Führer   Leader (Adolf Hitler). Hitler was the undisputed leader of the Nazi Party and enjoyed total power over the decision making within the Nazi Party.

Gau   District.

Gauleiter   District leader of the Nazi Party, and a very powerful figure within local Nazi Parties. As Hitler appointed each *Gauleiter*, he was able to exert important influence over local parties. After 1933, the Gauleiter system was added to the local government system in Nazi Germany.

Herrenvolk   Master race. The term was reserved for the supposed future 'racial elite' that would rule the Third Reich.

Hitler-Jugend   Hitler Youth. This organisation became a very important means of bringing young people into the Nazi Party. After 1933, the Hitler Youth became a key Nazi youth movement, which every young German was required to join.

KPD   The German Communist Party. The KPD took its ideas from Marx, but its orders from the leaders of the Soviet Union. The party refused to co-operate with the SPD, branding its members 'social fascists'. Many of its leaders thought that if Hitler was given power his incompetence could herald the end of the capitalist system in Germany and pave the way for the outbreak of a communist revolution.

Landstag   The legislature of each German regional state.

Lebensraum   Living space, a key concept in Hitler's foreign policy thinking. The idea was for the German armed forces not only to defeat the enemy but also to depopulate captured areas so that they could be used for the German population to expand into.

Mittelstand   Middle class. The middle class, usually the backbone of an effective democracy, suffered severe economic trauma during the 'great inflation' of 1923 and after the 1929 Wall Street crash. The middle class were always over-represented among Nazi members and voters, prompting one writer to describe Nazism as a 'revolt from the middle'.

Nationalsozialistische Deutsche Arbeiterpartei (NSDAP)   The National Socialist German Workers' Party, the full title of the Nazi Party. The party grew rapidly in support from 1928 onwards, to become the most popular political party in Germany at the time when Hitler came to power.

Reichsführer SS   Leader of the SS, the position occupied by Heinrich Himmler from 1929 to 1945. Himmler's racial anti-Semitism was to play a much more prominent role in the era of the Third Reich than in the period before 1933, when the SS was an elite security force whose principal aim was to protect Hitler at Nazi meetings.

Reichskanzler   Reich Chancellor.

Reichstag   German parliament. The Reichstag became increasingly powerless to save democracy, largely because of the increased use of Article 48 of the Weimar Constitution which allowed the President to bypass parliamentary rule as and when he thought there was an 'emergency'.

Reichswehr   The name of the Defensive Land Army created under the Weimar Republic (in 1935, it was renamed the Wehrmacht). The army played a very shady role during the Weimar period and was keen to support Hitler's rise to power, as many generals were anti-communist and saw the Nazis as allies in dealing with the communist threat and likely to support increased spending on the armed forces.

Schutzstaffel-SS   Hitler's black-shirted personal bodyguard, which grew into the most powerful Nazi organisation during the era of the Third Reich.

Sozialdemokratische Partei Deutschlands (SPD)   The Social Democratic Party. The SPD was the biggest supporter of Weimar democracy, but after 1928 it ceased to be involved in government, lost support from voters, and was ultimately powerless to prevent the collapse of democracy.

Stahlhelm   Steel Helmet, a leading nationalist ex-soldiers' organisation which operated during the Weimar era.

Sturmabteilungen (SA)   The Stormtroopers or 'Brownshirts', founded in 1921 as the private army of the Nazi Party, led by Ernst Roehm. Hitler viewed the SA as useful bully boys, but he did not feel they were an integral part of his racial elite and he refused to support the idea that the SA would play a leading role within the armed forces of the Third Reich.

Volk   Race. A central concept in Nazi ideology. Indeed, recent studies have shown just how integral racial ideas were within the Nazi elite.

Völkisch   Racial, ethnic, nationalist.

Völkischer Beobachter   *The Racial Observer*, the official Nazi Party newspaper. It is now known that secret army funds helped to finance the purchase of this newspaper.

Volksdeutsche   Ethnic Germans.

Volksgemeinschaft   The folk community. The Nazi slogan expressing the desire to create a classless, unified German society.

Zentrum   The Catholic Centre Party.

Amman, Max (1891–1957)   was born in Munich and met Hitler during his service in the army in the First World War. In 1921, he became the business manager of the Nazi Party. In 1922, he was appointed director of the party publishing house (Eher Verlag), which published *Mein Kampf*. He played a leading role in the management of the party newspaper (*Völkischer Beobachter*). After the fall of the Third Reich, Amman attempted to portray himself as a businessman with no real commitment to Nazism. In 1948, he was sentenced to ten years in a labour camp during the de-Nazification trials. He died in poverty in Munich in 1957.

Brüning, Heinrich (1885–1970)   German Chancellor from 1930 to 1932 and leader of the Catholic Centre Party. He led Germany at the height of the depression. His deflationary policies proved extremely unpopular. He resigned in May 1932. In 1934, he fled to Switzerland and then went to live in the USA, eventually becoming a professor of political science at Harvard University. He died in the USA in 1970.

Drexler, Anton (1884–1942)   A Munich locksmith who founded the German Workers' Party (DAP) in 1919, which subsequently turned into the Nazi Party. He viewed the DAP as a classless, popular party which espoused nationalism and was anti-capitalist, anti-Liberal and anti-Marxist. After Hitler took over the leadership of the Nazi Party, Drexler faded into the background and after 1924 never participated in the Nazi Party ever again. In February 1942, Drexler died a forgotten man.

Eckart, Dietrich (1868–1923)   A poet with a drinking problem. He was Hitler's first 'mentor', and was described by the Nazi leader as the spiritual godfather of the movement. Eckart helped to obtain the funds to buy the *Völkischer Beobachter*, and he introduced Hitler to several leading figures in the Bavarian upper class. Hitler dedicated *Mein Kampf* to Eckart. It is believed Eckart greatly influenced Hitler's developing anti-Semitism. Eckart's health was made worse by his alcoholism and his addiction to morphine. He died in 1923.

Feder, Gottfried (1883–1941)   The Nazi 'economic expert' during the early days of the party. Feder advocated the control of interest levied by banks. He helped to draft the 25-point Nazi Party programme. Yet Feder's anti-capitalist ideas were never adopted when the Nazi Party came to power, and he ceased to play a leading role in the party. He died in 1941 a forgotten figure.

Goebbels, Joseph (1897–1945)   The master spin doctor of the Nazi Party. He was unusual among the members of the early Nazi Party in that he held a doctorate, an academic qualification, which was despised by most leading Nazis who saw war medals as the best qualification for membership of the party. He suffered from polio in his childhood and had a club foot, which tormented him, especially during the era of the Third Reich, as it meant he did not match up physically as an ideal member of a master race. He started out on the 'socialist' wing of the Nazi Party and only became a key member of Hitler's elite after 1926. His sharp intelligence, his brilliant propaganda skills and his ideological passion for Nazism all served to make him a central figure in the Nazi Party. Goebbels was a violent anti-Semite, and he remained a deeply committed Nazi right up until his suicide in Hitler's bunker in Berlin in April 1945. His wife committed suicide with him after administering poison to all their six children.

Goering, Hermann (1893–1946)   A leading figure in the Nazi Party and the second most powerful figure in the Third Reich. He was a highly decorated pilot during the First World War, and his prestige as a war hero made him a leading and much admired figure in the early Nazi Party. In 1923, he took part in the Munich Beer Hall Putsch and was seriously wounded. He played a crucial role in Hitler's rise to power through his close relations with leading figures in the army. After Hitler came to power, Goering helped to create the Gestapo, the Nazi secret police, and later became commander of the Luftwaffe. On 9 May 1945, Goering was captured by American forces, and he was put on trial at Nuremberg in 1946. Two hours before his execution was due to take place for 'war crimes', he took a capsule of cyanide which he had hidden from his guards during his captivity.

Hess, Rudolf (1894–1987)   A leading figure in the early Nazi Party and deputy leader of the party. He took part in the Beer Hall Putsch and served his sentence in Landsberg fortress in 1923. From 1925 to 1932, he acted as Hitler's personal secretary. In May 1941, Hess flew to Britain on a 'peace mission', seemingly without the permission of Hitler, who declared him insane. He was sentenced to life imprisonment at the Nuremberg trials and spent the rest of his life in Spandau prison, guarded by the Russians, who refused to release him.

Hindenburg, Paul von (1847–1934)   President of Germany from 1925 to 1934 and the person who appointed Hitler as Chancellor in January 1933. He was a leading Prussian landowner and military figure and was a field marshal during the First World War. As President, he was supported by a coalition of nationalists, army commanders, aristocrats, conservatives and industrialists. After 1930, he used Article 48 of the constitution to appoint a series of right-wing figures who pushed Germany in an anti-democratic direction. Hindenburg remained President until his death in August 1934.

Hitler, Adolf (1889–1945)   The leader of the Nazi Party, the Führer of the German people during the era of the Third Reich, and one of the most significant figures in history. He was born in Branau am Inn, Austria, on 20 April 1889. He left school at sixteen without qualifications and spent time in Vienna and Munich before enlisting in the German army in 1914. He joined the German Workers' Party in 1919, which soon became the Nazi Party. His brilliant speeches were what brought him and the Nazi Party to prominence in German politics. He developed during the 1920s into a shrewd politician, and eventually persuaded Hindenburg to bring him to power. He turned Germany into a personal dictatorship. He committed suicide in his Berlin bunker in April 1945 having left Europe and Germany totally devastated.

Hugenberg, Alfred (1865–1951)   A press and film tycoon who led the German National People's Party (DNVP) from 1928 to 1933. He was a strong nationalist who had been a co-founder of the Pan-German League. He helped Hitler achieve national recognition during the campaign by the right against the Young Plan. He wanted to build a right-wing alliance with Hitler, but the Nazi leader refused to tie himself to someone he thought of as an 'old bourgeois Conservative'. Even so, Hugenberg supported Hitler coming to power, and the votes of the DNVP allowed the Nazis to pass the Enabling Act (1933), which paved the way for the creation of Nazi rule in Germany. After the war, Hugenberg was allowed to retain his property and business interests and he was not penalised by the de-Nazification courts. He died in 1951.

Ludendorff, Erich (1865–1937) was the virtual 'dictator' of Germany during the latter stages of the First World War. He played a prominent role in the Munich Beer Hall Putsch, even though he escaped prosecution. He ran for President in 1925, but received only 1.1 per cent of the vote. Relations between Hitler and Ludendorff deteriorated in the late 1920s. Even though he was never given a role in the Third Reich, he did receive a state funeral after his death in December 1937.

Papen, Franz von (1879–1969) was Chancellor of Germany in 1932 and played a leading role in helping Hitler gain power. After the Nazis came to power, Papen was made deputy Chancellor, but his influence over Hitler was minimal. In June 1934 he called for the Nazi leader to deal with 'extremists' in the SA. After the blood purge of the SA later the same month, Papen resigned, but he continued to serve Hitler's regime loyally. He was found not guilty of war crimes at the Nuremberg trial in 1946, but was sentenced to eight years in a labour camp in a de-Nazification trial a year later. Released in 1949, he wrote his memoirs in the early 1950s and died in 1969.

Roehm, Ernst (1887–1934) was the Chief of Staff of the SA and a leading figure in the early history of the party. After the Nazis came to power, Roehm expected the SA to be turned into a Nazi 'People's Army', but this idea was opposed by Hitler and the regular army. He was murdered in the blood purge, known as the 'Night of the Long Knives', in June 1934.

Rosenberg, Alfred (1893–1946) was the self-styled 'philosopher' of the early Nazi Party. He was a strong proponent of the idea that the Nazis had to create a 'master race' while in power or else Germany would cease to be a major force in the world. In 1934, he was given the grand title of 'The Führer's Delegate for the Entire Intellectual and Philosophical Education and Instruction of the National Socialist Party'. During the war, Rosenberg played a key part in seizing Jewish property in occupied territories. In June 1941, he was appointed Minister of the occupied eastern territories and was heavily involved in the implementation of the 'Final Solution' of the Jewish question. He was found guilty and hanged in October 1946, after being sentenced to death at the Nuremberg trials.

Schleicher, Kurt von (1882–1934) was the last German Chancellor of the Weimar Republic, but was only in power for 57 days. He wanted to institute a military dictatorship, but Hindenburg refused, and he was dismissed from office on 28 January 1933. Hitler never forgave him for attempting to prevent him from gaining power, and he was killed by the Nazis in June 1934 during the Night of the Long Knives.

Strasser, Gregor (1892–1934) was the leading figure in the north German wing of the Nazi Party before 1933. He supported many 'socialist' ideas such as bringing industry and land under state control and curbing the powers of banks and big business. He wanted the Nazi Party to gain support from the working classes and, because of this, he increasingly came into conflict with Hitler, as the party moved towards attracting the middle class and business groups in the early 1930s. He resigned from the party in December 1932 and left politics. He was murdered during the Night of the Long Knives on 30 June 1934.

Strasser, Otto (1897–1974)   was the younger brother of Gregor Strasser. He was a leading 'socialist' radical in the northern wing of the Nazi Party before 1933. His support for the 'socialist' parts of the programme brought him onto a collision course with Hitler. After refusing to accept the Nazi Party was anti-capitalist, he was expelled from the party in July 1930. After Hitler came to power, Strasser went into exile abroad. He died in Munich in August 1974.

REFERENCES

Place of publication is London unless otherwise stated.

Allen, W. (1995) *The Nazi Seizure of Power: The Experience of a Single German Town*. 2nd edn. Eyre and Spottiswoode.

Bullock, A. (1962) Hitler: *A Study in Tyranny*. Penguin.

Childers, T. (1983) *The Nazi Voter: The Social Foundations of Fascism in Germany, 1919–1933*. Chapel Hill, USA: University of North Carolina Press.

Fest, J. (1974) *Hitler*. Weidenfeld and Nicolson.

Fischer, C. (1995) *The Rise of the Nazis*. Manchester: Manchester University Press.

Geary, R. (1993) *Hitler and Nazism*. Routledge.

Hitler, A. (1938) *Mein Kampf*. Paternoster.

Kater, M. (1993) *The Nazi Party: A Social Profile of Members and Leaders, 1919–1945*. Oxford: Blackwell.

Kershaw, I. (2000) *The Nazi Dictatorship: Problems and Perspectives of Interpretation*. 4th edn. Edward Arnold.

Kershaw, I. (1998) *Hitler, 1889–1935: Hubris*. Allen Lane.

Kubizek, A. (1954) *Young Hitler*. Eyre and Spottiswoode.

Machtan, L. (2001) *The Hidden Hitler*. Perseus.

Mosse, G. (1966) *The Crisis of German Ideology: Intellectual Origins of the Third Reich*. Weidenfeld and Nicolson.

Muhlberger, D. (1991) *Hitler's Followers: Studies in the Sociology of the Nazi Movement*. Routledge.

Orlow, D. (1969) *The History of the Nazi Party: Vol. 1, 1919–1933*. Newton Abbot: David and Charles.

Payne, S. (1995) *A History of Fascism*. University College of London Press.

Shirer, W. (1961) *The Rise and Fall of the Third Reich*. Pan.

Toland, J. (1976) *Hitler*. Pan.

Waite, R. (1977) *The Psychopathic God: Adolf Hitler*. New York: Basic Books.

Zalampas, M. (1989) *Adolf Hitler and the Third Reich in American Magazines, 1923–1939*. Bowling Green, OH: Bowling Green State University Press.

BIBLIOGRAPHICAL ESSAY

The place of publication for all the books mentioned is London unless otherwise stated.

This very brief bibliographical essay is designed to provide some suggestions for further reading. The list is confined to books published in English. There is a wide range of studies on the rise to power of Adolf Hitler and the Nazi Party. The most outstanding collection of original documents, with a very good commentary, can be found in J. Noakes, and G. Pridham (eds.), *Nazism: A Documentary Reader*, Vol. 1: *The Rise to Power, 1919–1934* (Exeter: Exeter University Press, 1983–98), which contains some interesting documents from the years 1919–33. For a useful examination of the historical debate surrounding all aspects of the rise and fall of the Third Reich, see I. Kershaw, *The Nazi Dictatorship: Problems and Perspectives of Interpretation*, 4th edn (Edward Arnold, 2000).

There are many useful introductions to the subject, though most of these are focused on the Weimar Republic rather than specifically on the Nazi Party, most notably, M. Broszat, *Hitler and the Collapse of Weimar Germany* (Oxford: Berg, 1987); E. Eyck, *A History of the Weimar Republic*, 2 vols. (Wiley, 1967); E. Feuchtwanger, *From Weimar to Hitler* (Macmillan, 1993); J. Hiden, *The Weimar Republic*, 2nd edn (Longman, 1996); E. Kolb, *The Weimar Republic* (Unwin Hyman, 1988); A. J. Nicholls, *Weimar and the Rise of Hitler* (Macmillan, 1992); D. Peukert, *The Weimar Republic: The Crisis of Classical Modernity* (Allen Lane, 1991). All these studies attempt to explain the climate of politics in Weimar Germany and to weave the rise of the Nazis within a broader analytical framework.

For the impact of the Versailles settlement and the foreign policy debate in Germany during the Weimar era see: A. Adamthwaite, *The Lost Peace, 1918–1939: International Relations in Europe* (Edward Arnold, 1980); R. Henig, *Versailles and After* (Routledge, 1984); J. Hiden, *Germany and Europe, 1918–1939*, 2nd edn (Longman, 1993); J. Jacobson, *Locarno Diplomacy* (Princeton, NJ: Princeton University Press, 1972).

For the economic problems of the Weimar era, the following studies may be read with profit: R. Evans and D. Geary, *The German Unemployed, 1918–1936* (Croom Helm, 1987); N. Ferguson, *Paper and Iron: Hamburg Business and German Politics in the Era of Inflation, 1897–1927* (Cambridge: Cambridge University Press, 1995); W. Guttman, and P. Meehan, *The Great Inflation, 1923* (Farnborough: Saxon House, 1975); H. James, *The German Slump: Politics and Economics, 1924–1936* (Oxford: Oxford University Press, 1986); R. Overy, *The Nazi Economic Recovery* (Macmillan, 1982); J. Ringer, *The German Inflation of 1923* (Oxford: Oxford University Press, 1969); P. Stachura, (ed.), *Unemployment and the Great Depression in Weimar Germany* (Macmillan, 1987); H. Turner, *German Big Business and the Rise of Hitler* (Oxford: Oxford University Press, 1985).

For the role of the army in the politics of the Weimar era see: F. Carsten, *The Reichswehr and Politics, 1918–1933* (Oxford: Oxford University Press, 1966); H. Gordon, *The Reichswehr and the German Republic, 1919–1926* (Princeton NJ: Princeton University Press, 1957); J. Wheeler-Bennet, *Nemesis of Power: The German Army in Politics, 1918–1945* (Macmillan, 1961). For the various paramilitary groups that operated within Germany see: J. Diehl, *Paramilitary Politics in Weimar Germany* (Bloomington, IN: Indiana State University Press, 1977).

For information on the political parties in Weimar, the following studies are useful: R. Breitman, *German Socialism and Weimar Democracy* (Chapel Hill, NC: North Carolina Press, 1981); E. Evans, *The German Centre Party 1870–1933* (Chicago, IL: Illinois University Press, 1981); C. Fischer, *The German Communists and the Rise of Nazism* (Macmillan, 1991); W. Guttsmann, *The German Social Democratic Party, 1875–1933* (Allen and Unwin, 1981); L. Hertzmann, *DNVP-Right-wing Opposition in the Weimar Republic* (Lincoln, NE: Nebraska University Press, 1963); L. Jones, *Between Reform and Resistance. Studies in the History of German Conservatism from 1789 to 1945* (Oxford: Berg, 1993).

For the role played by President Hindenburg in the downfall of the Weimar Republic examine: A. Dorpalen, *Hindenburg and the Weimar Republic* (Princeton, NJ: Princeton University Press, 1964); J. Wheeler-Bennet, *Hindenburg: The Wooden Titan* (Macmillan, 1936).

There are also many useful studies which concentrate on the internal history of the Nazi Party before 1933, most notably C. Fischer, *The Rise of the Nazis* (Manchester: Manchester University Press, 1995), which not only provides some excellent insights into the supporters of Nazism, but also contains some good original documents. See also D. Orlow, *The History of the Nazi Party*, Vol. 1, 1919–1933 (Newton Abbot: David and Charles, 1973), which remains the standard work on the inner workings of the Nazi Party before 1933. For Nazi youth activism see: P. Stachura, *Nazi Youth in the Weimar Republic* (Clio Press, 1975).

Three useful micro studies of the Nazi Party at the local level before 1933 are: W. Allen, *The Nazi Seizure of Power: The Experience of a Single German Town, 1930–1935* (Eyre and Spottiswoode, 1966); J. Noakes, *The Nazi Party in Lower Saxony, 1921–1933* (Oxford: Oxford University Press, 1971); G. Pridham, *Hitler's Rise to Power: The Nazi Movement in Bavaria, 1923–1933* (Hart-Davis, 1973). The most exhaustive study of the membership of the Nazi Party remains M. Kater, *The Nazi Party: A Social Profile of Members and Leaders, 1919–1945* (Oxford: Blackwell, 1983). A recent study which takes issue with Kater's view of middle-class over-representation in the membership of the Nazi Party is D. Muhlberger, *Hitler's Followers: Studies in the Sociology of the Nazi Movement* (Routledge, 1991).

The two most useful studies of Nazi electoral support before 1933 are T. Childers, *The Nazi Voter: The Social Foundations of Fascism in Germany, 1919–1933* (Chapel Hill, NC: University of North Carolina Press, 1983) and R. Hamilton, *Who Voted For Hitler?* (Princeton, NC: Princeton University Press, 1982). See also T. Childers, (ed.), *The Foundations of the Nazi Constituency, 1919–1933* (Croom Helm, 1986).

Among the hundreds of biographies of Adolf Hitler, the best remains the brilliantly written and researched study by A. Bullock, *Hitler: A Study in Tyranny* (Penguin, 1962), which in spite of several competitors remains the most persuasive analysis of the Nazi dictator. The most recent attempt to sum up the life of the Nazi dictator is I. Kershaw, *Hitler, 1889–1935: Hubris* (Allen Lane, 1998), which offers some useful insights on Hitler in power and draws heavily on the already published document collections of Noakes and Pridham. A penetrating – and original – analysis of Hitler's early life and the rise to power of the Nazi Party can be found in J. Fest, *Hitler* (Weidenfeld and Nicolson, 1974), which examines the German archives in detail. See also W. Maser, *Hitler* (Allen Lane, 1973), J. Toland, *Adolf Hitler* (London, 1976), and N. Stone, *Hitler* (Hodder and Stoughton, 1980). For a psychological analysis of Hitler's life see R. Waite, *The Psychopathic God: Adolf Hitler* (New York: Basic Books, 1977).

For Nazi ideology see: R. Geary, *Hitler and Nazism* (Routledge, 1993), which provides some very penetrating insights; B. Lane and L. Rupp (eds.), *Nazi Ideology before 1933* (Manchester: Manchester University Press, 1978); S. Payne, *A History of Fascism* (University College of London Press, 1995); and G. Mosse, *The Crisis of German Ideology: Intellectual Origins of the Third Reich* (Weidenfeld and Nicolson, 1966).

INDEX

The Index includes everything except the Chronology, References and Bibliographical Essay. Locators in **bold** indicate definitions or explanations.

SEMINAR STUDIES IN HISTORY

General Editors: Clive Emsley & Gordon Martel

The series was founded by Patrick Richardson in 1966. Between 1980 and 1996 Roger Lockyer edited the series before handing over to Clive Emsley (Professor of History at the Open University) and Gordon Martel (Professor of International History at the University of Northern British Columbia, Canada and Senior Research Fellow at De Montfort University).

MEDIEVAL ENGLAND

The Pre-Reformation Church in England 1400–1530 (Second edition)
Christopher Harper-Bill   0 582 28989 0

Lancastrians and Yorkists: The Wars of the Roses
David R Cook   0 582 35384 X

Family and Kinship in England 1450–1800
Will Coster   0 582 35717 9

TUDOR ENGLAND

Henry VII (Third edition)
Roger Lockyer & Andrew Thrush   0 582 20912 9

Henry VIII (Second edition)
M D Palmer   0 582 35437 4

Tudor Rebellions (Fourth edition)
Anthony Fletcher & Diarmaid MacCulloch   0 582 28990 4

The Reign of Mary I (Second edition)
Robert Tittler   0 582 06107 5

Early Tudor Parliaments 1485–1558
Michael A R Graves   0 582 03497 3

The English Reformation 1530–1570
W J Sheils   0 582 35398 X

Elizabethan Parliaments 1559–1601 (Second edition)
Michael A R Graves   0 582 29196 8

England and Europe 1485–1603 (Second edition)
Susan Doran   0 582 28991 2

The Church of England 1570–1640
Andrew Foster   0 582 35574 5

STUART BRITAIN

Social Change and Continuity: England 1550-1750 (Second edition)
Barry Coward   0 582 29442 8

James I (Second edition)
S J Houston   0 582 20911 0

The English Civil War 1640-1649
Martyn Bennett   0 582 35392 0

Charles I, 1625-1640
Brian Quintrell   0 582 00354 7

The English Republic 1649-1660 (Second edition)
Toby Barnard   0 582 08003 7

Radical Puritans in England 1550-1660
R J Acheson   0 582 35515 X

The Restoration and the England of Charles II (Second edition)
John Miller   0 582 29223 9

The Glorious Revolution (Second edition)
John Miller   0 582 29222 0

EARLY MODERN EUROPE

The Renaissance (Second edition)
Alison Brown   0 582 30781 3

The Emperor Charles V
Martyn Rady   0 582 35475 7

French Renaissance Monarchy: Francis I and Henry II (Second edition)
Robert Knecht   0 582 28707 3

The Protestant Reformation in Europe
Andrew Johnston   0 582 07020 1

The French Wars of Religion 1559-1598 (Second edition)
Robert Knecht   0 582 28533 X

Phillip II
Geoffrey Woodward   0 582 07232 8

The Thirty Years' War
Peter Limm   0 582 35373 4

Louis XIV
Peter Campbell   0 582 01770 X

Spain in the Seventeenth Century
Graham Darby   0 582 07234 4

Peter the Great
William Marshall   0 582 00355 5

EUROPE 1789–1918

Britain and the French Revolution
Clive Emsley   0 582 36961 4

Revolution and Terror in France 1789–1795 (Second edition)
D G Wright   0 582 00379 2

Napoleon and Europe
D G Wright   0 582 35457 9

The Abolition of Serfdom in Russia 1762–1907
David Moon   0 582 29486 X

Nineteenth-Century Russia: Opposition to Autocracy
Derek Offord   0 582 35767 5

The Constitutional Monarchy in France 1814–48
Pamela Pilbeam   0 582 31210 8

The 1848 Revolutions (Second edition)
Peter Jones   0 582 06106 7

The Italian Risorgimento
M Clark   0 582 00353 9

Bismarck & Germany 1862–1890 (Second edition)
D G Williamson   0 582 29321 9

Imperial Germany 1890–1918
Ian Porter, Ian Armour and Roger Lockyer   0 582 03496 5

The Dissolution of the Austro-Hungarian Empire 1867–1918 (Second edition)
John W Mason   0 582 29466 5

Second Empire and Commune: France 1848–1871 (Second edition)
William H C Smith   0 582 28705 7

France 1870–1914 (Second edition)
Robert Gildea   0 582 29221 2

The Scramble for Africa (Second edition)
M E Chamberlain   0 582 36881 2

Late Imperial Russia 1890–1917
John F Hutchinson   0 582 32721 0

The First World War
Stuart Robson   0 582 31556 5

Austria, Prussia and Germany 1806–1871
John Breuilly   0 582 43739 3

EUROPE SINCE 1918

The Russian Revolution (Second edition)
Anthony Wood   0 582 35559 1

Lenin's Revolution: Russia 1917–1921
David Marples   0 582 31917 X

Parliamentary Reform in Britain c. 1770–1918
Eric J Evans   0 582 29467 3

Democracy and Reform 1815–1885
D G Wright   0 582 31400 3

Poverty and Poor Law Reform in Nineteenth-Century Britain 1834–1914:
From Chadwick to Booth
David Englander   0 582 31554 9

The Birth of Industrial Britain: Economic Change 1750–1850
Kenneth Morgan   0 582 29833 4

Chartism (Third edition)
Edward Royle   0 582 29080 5

Peel and the Conservative Party 1830–1850
Paul Adelman   0 582 35557 5

Gladstone, Disraeli and later Victorian Politics (Third edition)
Paul Adelman   0 582 29322 7

Britain and Ireland: From Home Rule to Independence
Jeremy Smith   0 582 30193 9

TWENTIETH-CENTURY BRITAIN

The Rise of the Labour Party 1880–1945 (Third edition)
Paul Adelman   0 582 29210 7

The Conservative Party and British Politics 1902–1951
Stuart Ball   0 582 08002 9

The Decline of the Liberal Party 1910–1931 (Second edition)
Paul Adelman   0 582 27733 7

The British Women's Suffrage Campaign 1866–1928
Harold L Smith   0 582 29811 3

War & Society in Britain 1899–1948
Rex Pope   0 582 03531 7

The British Economy since 1914: A Study in Decline?
Rex Pope   0 582 30194 7

Unemployment in Britain between the Wars
Stephen Constantine   0 582 35232 0

The Attlee Governments 1945–1951
Kevin Jefferys   0 582 06105 9

The Conservative Governments 1951–1964
Andrew Boxer   0 582 20913 7

Britain under Thatcher
Anthony Seldon and Daniel Collings   0 582 31714 2

Britain and Empire 1880–1945
Dane Kennedy   0 582 41493 8

INTERNATIONAL HISTORY

The Eastern Question 1774–1923 (Second edition)
A L Macfie   0 582 29195 X

India 1885–1947: The Unmaking of an Empire
Ian Copland   0 582 38173 8

The Origins of the First World War (Second edition)
Gordon Martel   0 582 28697 2

The United States and the First World War
Jennifer D Keene   0 582 35620 2

Women and the First World War
Susan R Grayzel   0 582 41876 3

Anti-Semitism before the Holocaust
Albert S Lindemann   0 582 36964 9

The Origins of the Cold War 1941–1949 (Third edition)
Martin McCauley   0 582 77284 2

Russia, America and the Cold War 1949–1991
Martin McCauley   0 582 27936 4

The Arab–Israeli Conflict
Kirsten E Schulze   0 582 31646 4

The United Nations since 1945: Peacekeeping and the Cold War
Norrie MacQueen   0 582 35673 3

Decolonisation: The British Experience since 1945
Nicholas J White   0 582 29087 2

WORLD HISTORY

China in Transformation 1900–1949
Colin Mackerras   0 582 31209 4

Japan Faces the World 1925–1952
Mary L Hanneman   0 582 36898 7

Japan in Transformation 1952–2000
Jeff Kingston   0 582 41875 5

China since 1949
Linda Benson   0 582 35722 5

US HISTORY

American Abolitionists
Stanley Harrold   0 582 35738 1

The American Civil War 1861–1865
Reid Mitchell   0 582 31973 0

America in the Progressive Era 1890–1914
Lewis L Gould

The United States and the First World War
Jennifer D Keene

The Truman Years 1945–1953
Mark S Byrnes

The Korean War
Steven Hugh Lee

The Origins of the Vietnam War
Fredrik Logevall

The Vietnam War
Mitchell Hall

American Expansionism 1783–1860
Mark S Joy

The United States and Europe in the Twentieth Century
David Ryan

0 582 35671 7

0 582 35620 2

0 582 32904 3

0 582 31988 9

0 582 31918 8

0 582 32859 4

0 582 36965 7

0 582 30864 X